Seen,
Secure,
Free

Seen, Secure, Free

*How a Life Hidden with Christ
Strengthens and Transforms You*

ALLISON ALLEN

W PUBLISHING GROUP

AN IMPRINT OF THOMAS NELSON

Seen, Secure, Free

© 2024 Allison Allen

Published in Nashville, Tennessee, by W Publishing, an imprint of Thomas Nelson.

Author represented by Lisa Jackson of Alive Literary Agency.

Thomas Nelson titles may be purchased in bulk for educational, business, fundraising, or sales promotional use. For information, please email SpecialMarkets@ThomasNelson.com.

Unless otherwise noted, Scripture quotations are taken from the Holy Bible, New International Version®, NIV®. Copyright © 1973, 1978, 1984, 2011 by Biblica, Inc.® Used by permission of Zondervan. All rights reserved worldwide. www.zondervan.com. The "NIV" and "New International Version" are trademarks registered in the United States Patent and Trademark Office by Biblica, Inc.®

Scripture quotations marked ASV are taken from the American Standard Version. Public domain.

Scripture quotations marked BSB are taken from the Holy Bible, Berean Study Bible, BSB. Copyright © 2016, 2018 by Bible Hub. Used by permission. All rights reserved worldwide.

Scripture quotations marked CEV are taken from the Contemporary English Version. Copyright © 1991, 1992, 1995 by American Bible Society. Used by permission.

Scripture quotations marked CSB are taken from the Christian Standard Bible®. Copyright © 2017 by Holman Bible Publishers. Used by permission. Christian Standard Bible® and CSB® are federally registered trademarks of Holman Bible Publishers.

Scripture quotations marked ESV are taken from the ESV® Bible (The Holy Bible, English Standard Version®). Copyright © 2001 by Crossway, a publishing ministry of Good News Publishers. Used by permission. All rights reserved.

Scripture quotations marked NKJV are taken from the New King James Version®. Copyright © 1982 by Thomas Nelson. Used by permission. All rights reserved.

Italics added to Scripture quotations are the author's emphasis.

Some names and identifying details have been changed to protect the privacy of the individuals involved.

Any internet addresses, phone numbers, or company or product information printed in this book are offered as a resource and are not intended in any way to be or to imply an endorsement by Thomas Nelson, nor does Thomas Nelson vouch for the existence, content, or services of these sites, phone numbers, companies, or products beyond the life of this book.

ISBN 9781400339372 (audiobook)
ISBN 9781400339365 (eBook)
ISBN 9781400339358 (SC)

Library of Congress Control Number: 2023941251

Printed in the United States of America

24 25 26 27 28 LBC 5 4 3 2 1

For Beach-walkers, doggedly searching for signs
of God's goodness in the wild storm
For Along-siders, stubbornly showing up with grace
in their mouths and strength in their hands

Contents

Contents

PART 3: FREE

Introduction

Hey there, fellow sojourner.

I'm so grateful you're here. I understand that in a world with an ocean full of ocean-sized things to occupy one's time, the gift of your time is just that—a gift.

I wish we had five minutes standing side by side, staring out at the ocean, watching the waves hurl themselves upon the shore. I know I'd wonder about the state of your heart. Maybe it's rested and rejoicing. Maybe it's in need of renovation. Maybe it's shouldering rejection or tainted with a residue you wish the surf could scrub off. Maybe your heart is just exhausted and frail.

I get it, friend.

Before I go on, let me introduce myself. I'm Allison, a tall girl who has stood on some stages, written some books, and spoken some words. I love my Tall Man; my two old- and new-covenant sons, Levi and Luke; and all my people. I'm smitten with the bride of Christ, and I think our weaknesses attract His glory more than our strengths ever could. I'm a woman who has experienced God's love at the bottom of the well and at the ceiling of the sky. And I've had times when my heart's been wrecked and worn out and every-thing in between.

I so get it.

Our hearts may have been shaped by different storms, but I bet all the fish in the sea that the same things drive them to their proverbial knees and cause the same longing.

I bet both of our hearts love Jesus, yet we have a suspicion that we've allowed the world's pressure to make ourselves visible—to "make a name for ourselves"—to creep in as well, and it can distract us and dampen our delight in Him.

We love Jesus and know that He does not call us to an unending, pressured performance but to something more rooted and enduring than we could dream.

We love Jesus and are exhausted from being driven by the opinions of others, the voices of the crowd, rather than the voice of the King.

We love Jesus and want to rediscover the delight of the hidden-with-Christ life, remembering that He is our security.

We love Jesus and want to be released back into the story He is writing.

We love Jesus and want to sink our hearts into the relief that comes from knowing we are seen by God.

We crave security and freedom way down deep, where rot and decay can never invade.

Not long ago, I was desperately in need of that security and freedom—I didn't even know how much—and God led me to the sands of the Outer Banks to show me that need and to fulfill it. He reminded me of eternal truths I so easily forget.

Introduction

As someone who has spent a good portion of her life as an actor, there is a terrible tendency in me to equate activity with authentic existence. Visibility with validity. Fame with favor. Though I am not proud of it, there are times I confuse making a name for myself (with all the spiritual bells and whistles attached, of course) with lifting high the name of Jesus. When others don't seem to see me, I can struggle to remember my worth. When I surrender to the allure of shiny, worldly things, I can be infested with insecurity.

I can allow my heart to be slyly twisted—focusing on lesser loves, valuing lesser things. I chase hard after them and then wonder why my tank is empty. Where's the joy? The power, vision, and hope? The security and freedom?

But eventually—often after a storm—I stop, search God's horizon, and see there the great call of the gospel rising afresh like the morning sun, and I remember:

Hide yourself in the finished work of the cross, heart.

Find joy in the hidden life, heart.

Remember Jesus' call is not about jockeying to be seen by the world, heart. This clarion call invites you to collapse into the knowledge of how deeply seen you are by the Father.

His love will break your heart of stone and make it new with soft flesh and endurance.

I've lived that journey this past year on the stormy beaches of my life. I've meandered through some of the lesser-known, concealed characters of Scripture and the lessons of Colossians and found myself in a place of surprising beauty and strength.

I'm ready to walk with you along this path. Let's get sand between our toes. Let's run the beach together and look to the One who is ever and always bringing deeper transformation and freedom.

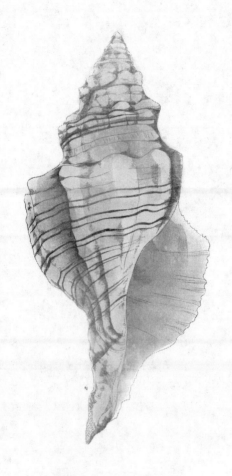

Seen

PART 1

CHAPTER 1

Discovered

The eyes of the LORD are everywhere.

PROVERBS 15:3

In the year of our desolation, we went to the Outer Banks. For a quarter of a century, my family had traveled the long distance from our home each summer to gather at the blustery barrier islands off the east coast of North Carolina, lovingly known as the Outer Banks. Dotted by towns with inscrutable names like Nags Head and Kill Devil Hills, the Outer Banks had been a bastion of refuge for us, and, until the area was made popular by the Netflix series, relatively few knew of the Banks's secluded beaches, rough edges, and comforts. Its nature and nurture had been kept somewhat secret, like a schoolgirl's crush.

For twenty-four summers we had walked the bends of those beaches, our feet learning where the unpredictable Atlantic waters were likely to break on the hidden shoreline, stepping around sinking sand, searching for sand that was sturdy.

In our twenty-fifth summer, however, we weren't sure if anything was sturdy any longer; our sails had been shot through. We felt frail and anchorless in the sea's squall. Calling, ministry, relationships, direction—the masts of our lives were bending in the strong winds. During those desperate days, every feeling was sharp, like the sting of salty sea spray on a frigid gust. We endured crashing wave upon wave.

And yet.

When I finally quieted down and noticed the power of the wind more than my own powerlessness in the storm, I felt Another walking alongside my pain. I recognized Him, sensed His steadying arm, and suspected He was extending an invitation—a gentle offer that contrasted with the savage storm rolling around the seabed of my heart. Jesus' invitation was soft and quiet, a countermelody to the wild tumult, a soothing lullaby sung over the storm. I recognized it as a hymn from a heavenly country, one He'd been inviting me to sing for a very long while.

During those days of emotional turbulence, I couldn't quite grasp His tune as I stepped along the shore, but I longed for it like a child who hopes to hear the tide in a conch shell.

Early on the last day of our beach retreat, my husband and I combed the sandy contours one last time. Halfway into our walk, as we stepped along the surf's break, I suddenly recoiled, trying to avoid stepping on the decaying coil of a brown puffer fish. At least, that's what I thought it was. Peering at the object more closely, I called to my husband, "Hey! That's a shell! A whole shell!" His disbelief matched mine as we bent over, wide-eyed, to scoop up the sea's gift.

At face value, our incredulity might seem dramatic. After all, shells regularly litter beaches. But not usually *whole* shells like this one. Not on the Outer Banks. At least, not that I've found during my beachcombing seasons there. The frigid Atlantic waters are so fierce and unruly that any shell making landfall is usually fractured, a fragmented former self.

And I'd never, in all my life, felt as much like a fragmented shell as I did then.

Until that day, the complete shells I had found on my beachcombing expeditions had been small to medium in size with typical coloring. But this was a different specimen altogether. It was almost the length of my hand, and its whorls were lovely and dark, with streaks of black, gray, and yellow that seemed to be brushed upon its curling contours. Whelk shells are usually milky, but this one looked as if a midnight sky had been reduced into one of nature's most delicate husks, rounded out by a perfect band of stars—as if an Impressionist master had daubed and brushed a paintbrush upon it. In all my years, I'd never seen anything like it.

I carried the rare shell back to our beach house, cradled in my hands like a piece of sea glass.

We showed our treasure from the sea to our family, and everyone had a similar reaction to the whelk shell's whole state. Jetta, my mother-in-law, commented on its unusual color as I was already surfing the world's digital library to sleuth out what could have caused the odd markings. What I found caught me up short: "Black-stained shells have been buried in the mud for hundreds, if not thousands, of years. They make their way to the beach after being dug up by dredging."[1]

This seashell had likely been buried for centuries, if not millennia, and its beautiful colors and complete form were due to its deep concealment in the sand and sediment.[2]

In that moment I realized I was not hidden from God's sight. I was not forgotten. I was discoverable. I was seen.

Later that day, Jetta said, "You know, the shell is you."

I didn't say anything that I recall. Odd—as words are usually my defense against feeling. Torrents and torrents of words, trying to drown a thing determined to float.

After pressing down the pain of that season for so long, my heart finally began to exhale. In that moment I realized I was not hidden from God's sight. I was not forgotten.

I was discoverable.

I was seen.

The Beauty of Hiddenness

My mother-in-law's words that day crystallized something I'd been trying to put my spiritual finger on for a long time, that ancient melody on the currents: the invitation to and the glory of a life hidden with Christ in God. To me, the shell represented all of that.

The shell was *beautiful* because it had been hidden.

The shell was *protected* because it had been hidden.

The shell was *whole* because it had been hidden.

During the following days, a boatload of questions rose to the top of my mind:

- *What does it really mean to be hidden?*
- *In a world that equates being seen with significance, and excellence with exposure, what does it mean to choose a life "hidden with Christ in God," as Paul penned in Colossians 3:3?*
- *How can I help my stubborn heart comprehend that the hidden life may, indeed, be a better life—even a transformational life?*
- *As a companion of Christ, why do I so often run from the holy hiddenness He offers me and instead pursue the world's visibility?*
- *Why do I feel driven to be seen by the world rather than to revel in the knowledge of being seen by the One who sees me?*
- *What can I learn from the stories of the concealed characters and hidden heroes of the faith?*
- *Are there any downsides to hiddenness?*
- *Is there a time when choosing concealment is not Christlike but cowardly?*
- *How can I remain in the positional reality of being hidden with Christ while stepping out in the great adventure with Him?*

These questions seemed new and yet somehow ancient. The swirling interrogatives invited me to examine the tectonic plates of my spiritual life. To test for soundness and notice the fault lines. To ask and continue to ask—circling these questions like an osprey circling the nest. To look for other living parables of hiddenness, like the story of the black whelk.

In the weeks that followed, that moment of finding the shell continued to surface in the waters of my life. I started examining the Scriptures for instances of hiddenness. I looked back at my past writing life in theatre and previous talks I had given, noticing how often I had focused on biblical characters who were unknown and unheralded. The secondaries. The tertiaries. Ensemble members.

Supporting roles. There I found an ongoing theme of living without the pressure to make something of oneself, living without fighting to be seen, living reoriented to the heartbeat of the gospel. Could it be that God had been surreptitiously kneading this truth into my heart for years?

This is why I mentioned that it felt as if an ancient melody called to me over the tumult on the beach that day. Jesus had been singing the song for eons, and pain has a way of making a gal finally cup her ears to try to catch the melody.

I figured if I really sat with it, maybe wrote it out, even, I'd begin to fully grasp it. So I began. Click-clacking the keys, petitioning God for a glimpse of His heart regarding a countercultural, quieter, gentler way of living—one that might transform and strengthen me. Strengthen us. And as I ruminated on the shell, it became a full picture of the beauty and bounty of hiddenness I was discovering in Scripture.

In *Seen, Secure, Free*, we'll lean into the lessons of Scripture, sitting with the transformative power of the hidden-with-Christ life (Colossians 3:3). We'll glean from some "Concealed Characters" in God's epic love story, letting those hidden heroes of Scripture invite us into a life of contentment and wide-eyed wonder.

One of Many Others

Let's make our way toward our first Concealed Character in Luke 8:1–3, where we find a group of women in first-century Israel participating in something that would have been completely countercultural for that day and age:

Afterward he [Jesus] was traveling from one town and village to another, preaching and telling the good news of the kingdom of God. The Twelve were with him, and *also some women who had been healed of evil spirits and sicknesses*: Mary, called Magdalene (seven demons had come out of her); Joanna the wife of Chuza, Herod's steward; Susanna; *and many others who were supporting them from their possessions.* (CSB)

The fact that these women were not only following an itinerant Jewish rabbi who preached the good news of the kingdom of God but also supporting Jesus and His crew from their own bank accounts is an upending surprise.

New Testament scholar Craig Keener put it this way: "For these women to travel with the group would have been viewed as scandalous, at least by Jesus' detractors. Apart from some small Greek philosophic schools, adult coeducation was unheard of, and that these women are learning Jesus' teaching as closely as his male disciples would surely bother some outsiders as well. . . . We know of no other women disciples among Jewish teachers in this period."[3]

I sometimes wonder who in the dickens these "many others" were who gladly spent their sustenance on the Son of God. Exactly who comprised this group of women who had been released from the thumb of the Enemy, hidden without earthly notoriety in this scripture? Whoever they were, they chose to spend themselves and their God-given resources on the One who matters most—and will for eternity.

Below, I imagine what one of these anonymous women's stories might sound like had she shared it firsthand.

CONCEALED CHARACTERS

One of Many Others

I was not always one given to many words. Though they are friends to me now, I remember a time before their presence, recalling the worried looks that twisted my parents' brows and the earnest petitions of the priests when I was long past the time of speech—yet no speech came. I could purse my lips around the shape of a sound; I could comprehend words; I could construct worlds from them inside my mind, but no matter how hard I pursed my lips, no sound followed. The sounds I heard instead were the taunts of others: *mute, dumb, demon-possessed.* Mine was a life parents used as a threat to scare their children into behaving.

I longed for a life of hiddenness—one of protection, not exhibition—so I stayed inside, weaving as my mother had, and her mother before her. My mother would cluck as she passed me at work, saying, "You weave as fast as swallow wings beat. No one's work surpasses yours." I longed to say, "Thank you, Mama." I longed to say anything—any word—but I had long since quit trying.

I wove this deep longing into every grand banqueting basket and small fig bowl. My skill in weaving (if not my silence) brought me to the notice of Chuza, the steward of Herod's chaotic household. My baskets were prized for their sturdiness and unusual, crisscrossed patterns. I was paid handsomely for my craftsmanship—I am not ashamed of this because of what that money was one day used for.

In those days I could move freely about the palace; my muteness was too easily mistaken for deafness. But just because I did not speak did not mean I did not hear. In particular, I greedily listened for the voice of the one they called John the Baptizer. Often Herod, son of the Great, sat with the wild prophet—and this even after John had baldly rebuked the king to his corpulent face for wedding his own brother's wife. The king listened to the voice of the desert, who proclaimed that the Coming One Who Had Come would topple the kingdoms of the world like stacked dice and that Herod was only a crowned pawn in the hand of God. How does one prophesy as boldly in prison as upon a podium?

I often lingered longer than necessary, listening to their conversations while clearing the emptied baskets. On the last night of the spring moon, I caught the eye of the prophet. He looked back at me, the corners of his cracked mouth turned up in a smile. Not as mad as they whispered. Not as mean either. And not long for the earth.

I often wonder now if Joanna, the wife of Herod's steward, had witnessed me lingering, ingesting the Baptizer's words with hunger. Whatever the reason, this woman of wealth and status asked me to journey with her. She had acquired permission from her husband for me to be gone, so I made ready as quickly as I could. She must've seen the question in my worried eyes. "A gathering" is all she said, motioning for me to hurry up.

As we traveled many long hours, Joanna began to unfold her words—many of the same refrains as John the prophet: the Coming One had come, she said. We have seen Him, she said. As the breeze of Galilee's sea cooled me down, I mused, *What kind of man is this?*

I heard Him before I saw Him—and then I saw Him.

Seen, Secure, Free

Gathered at His feet were men and women together. I had never seen such a thing in the light of day. I came closer, like a child discovering a hidden treasure. The One Joanna called Jesus stopped teaching, looked at me, and said firmly, "Speak." There was such power in His single word I'm surprised the rocks themselves didn't burst into poetry.

My first words were sobs. My voice was higher than I imagined. Younger, somehow.

My own speech was returned to me by the One who spoke the world into existence. And I could finally say, "Thank You, thank You, thank You," like a child's ditty.

From that day onward, I followed Him, as I could. With Joanna. With Susanna. With Mary of Magdala. With many others who had been healed as I had been. Joanna never wasted her words or her resources; she used every coin, every vestige of strength to support the work of Jesus and to convince others the Messiah had come.

Not long afterward, John, the great voice of the desert, would be taken from us. And then Jesus, the great Voice of the kingdom, would be taken as well—the cross would silence the Voice that sang the world into being. But three days later, He would rise and sing, never to be silenced again. The refrain of the church would crescendo into an unstoppable sound. Even Manaen of Herod's household would join it. The song grew louder with each new voice.

I am among the "many others" listed in scrolls. I never desired more than this. Hidden from history, hidden in His story. Some sought a name for themselves, even among His own disciples, but I was happy to have none of it. In some way, my name no longer mattered once He gave me back my voice. I am content to

10

be known as one of many others, a word in a sentence, a thread in a garment, a grain of sand on the shore.

I am happily unknown and unseen to all others, if only known and seen by Him.[4]

Turn the Tapestry

One of many others.

A grain of sand upon the shore.

For much of my life, I was a professional actor. During my years onstage, including almost 650 performances of *Grease* on Broadway, I've had some gripping moments: corsets so tight I thought I might cough up a lung, slips and trips that would make Lucille Ball look like a prima ballerina, forgotten lines, unexpected triumphs, and even going on as an understudy in the middle of a show. You name it, and I've probably lived it on the stage.

Several years back, however, something occurred that took the theatrical cake in terms of one of the themes we're circling: hiddenness.

Because our lead had suddenly fallen ill, I had to step in to play a role I had never played before in a ministry production; there was no understudy. I didn't know the lines by heart, even though I had cowritten the piece. The lead was a petite blonde, and I'm a five-foot-twelve brunette; I've never been called "petite" in all my life. One of these things was decidedly not like the other. But what could be done? It was either let the show go on or bring down the curtain and say amen.

I carted the script onstage in a huge notebook, the pages flipping like condor wings. And off we went. People were assigned backstage to move me from one exit to the next entrance. You may not know this, but often the complex choreography onstage has nothing on the flurry of activity backstage. Imagine that a beautiful tapestry is visible to the audience, while the flip side is the backstage experience—overlapping and chaotic, performers bobbing and weaving hither and yon. That night, the backstage choreography for me was especially gnarled, like tangled yarns. At the final company bow almost two hours later, I felt knotted up inside, hanging by a proverbial thread.

Reflecting on my experience, I realize the part I played that night is memorialized . . . exactly nowhere. Not in any cast list. Not in any program. And certainly not on film. Though I was seen by the audience members, I was hidden from accolades or notoriety. And, frankly, I didn't give it a second thought because my thoughts and energy were poured into a bigger task. In that unusual moment, nothing mattered more than the story. Receiving credit was not a main consideration. Having kudos, attagirls, or gold stars was an afterthought compared to the thrill of being a small part of something so much larger than myself. Of contributing. Of living as a part of *we* instead of just *me*.

There's a healing quality to that, I think—a sort of coming home to the communal spaces we were created to inhabit. A place where we are healthier, safely seen, and able to experience the joy of being *a part* rather than apart.

Years ago, I was asked to compose a dramatic reading using

every "one another" in Scripture: verses in which we are commanded and encouraged to live the gospel in close relationships. The phrase occurs more than fifty times in the Bible, which meant the script was long and took a good spate of time for the actors to read. I remember standing in the back of the sanctuary while the words of the Bible rang out.

Love one another.
Forgive one another.
Bear with one another.
Be devoted to one another.
Honor one another.
Build one another.
Teach one another.
Comfort one another.
Exhort one another.
Speak to one another.
Be patient with one another.
Accept one another.

These active, reciprocal phrases remind my heart that nothing is as glorious, or as necessary, as the community of the body of Christ. This is the only place we can practice, prove, and progress in these biblical virtues. Gathered together. Connected. Where we can be part of a whole.

My hidden, unexpected turn onstage that night emphasized this reality for me and became a living parable for my oh-so-prone-to-get-it-wrong, wonky heart. My primary focus was embodying and supporting the story, credit or not. In the end, having my name be "unnamed" was barely a consideration. And surprisingly,

I found an enduring gift in the whole process: a deeper trust and dependence on God in my hiddenness.

I want to take that delightful understanding with me every day, whether standing in front of hundreds or living in obscurity.

Life with Christ, among a million other glorious realities, is rooted in the posture of the heart—and the posture of the heart often determines the progress of the soul. So when you and I feel the pressure to posture and perform, let's come back to what we were made for and ask God to shape in us a "one-of-many-others" heart.

Another Other

Scripture is replete with one-of-many-others hearts. Let's take a walk back into the Old Testament story of Nehemiah, when the Jewish exiles were back in Israel after decades of Babylonian captivity. Even after years of being back in their homeland, much of the important rebuilding work had been left undone. Now, under the leadership of Nehemiah, the people were commanded to shore up the walls of protection around Jerusalem despite incredible ridicule and recrimination.

Nehemiah 3 features an extensive cast list of those who did (and did not) take part in the holy work of restoration and rebuilding. One group stands in the spotlight. Verse 12 says, "Shallum son of Hallohesh, ruler of a half-district of Jerusalem, repaired the next section *with the help of his daughters*." The daring daughters of Shallum helped their father rebuild the wall. I imagine these daughters were women of renown due to their father's status as ruler of a half-district of Jerusalem; they might have easily opted out of manual labor. But there they were—the only women listed among the workers—baring their biceps, helping to heave-ho those great stones or clear debris. These women raised their hands and hearts to be a part of the restoration of the wall, and, more importantly, the restoration of the heritage of God's people.[5]

The daughters of Shallum—what were their names? I wish I knew; I know only that they were faithful.

And what of the epilogue of Hebrews 11, often called the "Hall of Faith"? It issues this resounding tribute to unnamed believers:

> Women received back their dead, raised to life again. There were others who were tortured, refusing to be released so that they might gain an even better resurrection. Some faced jeers and flogging, and even chains and imprisonment. They were put to death by stoning; they were sawed in two; they were killed by the sword. They went about in sheepskins and goatskins, destitute, persecuted and mistreated—the world was not worthy of them. They wandered in deserts and mountains, living in caves and in holes in the ground. These were all commended for their faith, yet none of them received what had been promised. (vv. 35–39)

We might have expected the writer of Hebrews to build up to a big finish, possibly ending with someone like Abraham, Joseph, or Moses. Our human tendency is to strain toward the literary climax, to finish with the spotlight on the biggest star—the spiritual celebrity, if you will. Yet here we witness the upside-down ethos of the kingdom, a holy counterpoint to the way we humans so often define worth and validity. After running through a who's who of the titans of the faith, this chapter concludes with hidden, anonymous "women" and "others."

> **In the end, the great story of the kingdom doesn't conclude with the famous; it concludes with the faithful.**

What were their names? I wish I knew; I know only that they were faithful.

In the end, the great story of the kingdom doesn't conclude with the famous; it concludes with the faithful.

Oh, to have a heart like that! A heart that is surrendered to His Spirit. A heart that seeks and delights in being a hidden part of His story.

I long to hear God say to me, as He said to King Cyrus, "I will give you hidden treasures [or *the treasures of darkness* in other translations], riches stored in secret places, so that you may know that I am the LORD, the God of Israel, who summons you by name" (Isaiah 45:3). One scholar described these treasures as "those that are the most carefully hidden, as being the most precious."[6] Precious, hidden blessings of the material sort awaited King Cyrus, who was chosen by God to be the deliverer of Israel. And it is no less true for us, though the blessings we receive are spiritual. The apostle Paul wrote, "Blessed is the God and Father of our Lord Jesus Christ, who has blessed us with every spiritual blessing in the heavens in Christ" (Ephesians 1:3 CSB). Hope. Provision. Wisdom. The list could go on forever.

Scripture even records that our High Priest, Jesus, lives to make intercession for us (Hebrews 7:25). Think on that. You never live an unprayed-for day in your life. Jesus has you covered. When you feel like everything is shaking, remember that right now in heaven, the Author and Finisher of your faith is praying that your faith may not fail. What an astonishing reality!

God has stored up for us every untold blessing as we pursue

the hidden-with-Christ life, where everything we will ever need has been purchased and procured by the life and work of Christ.

As it is so often stated, *GRACE* is God's Riches at Christ's Expense. As humans, we have difficulty comprehending the vastness of God's riches or Christ's expense. But as we begin to apprentice our hearts to this gospel-centric truth, we are set free from the driving pressure to perform. As children of the promise, we cannot add one iota to what Jesus has eternally accomplished for us. Jesus composes the story. Sings the final note. Takes the final bow. All the spit-shined performances in the world cannot contribute to His perfect work of salvation. This relieves, resets, and rests me; I can rest in knowing to the core that I am seen by Him.

We are seen by the God of the universe.

Our worth, our beauty, is in the eye of the Beholder.

Knowing this secures us and frees us. It changes our focus in life and catapults us into the glorious freedom of children of God. And, most delightfully, this fresh perspective sets us free to join Him in work that lasts for all eternity.

So much of the emotional energy we spend on struggling to be seen—by peers, the internet, the world, or whoever/whatever—could be poured instead into the lasting goodness of the gospel. Like "some others" who are listed in Scripture, we can set our minds and eyes on a city "whose architect and builder is God" Himself (Hebrews 11:10). We can invest ourselves in seeking first the kingdom of God. (Anyone else humming the beautiful worship song from the '70s and '80s?) We can live like people whose treasures are hidden in heaven, where nothing can denigrate them (Matthew 6:19–20).

We can delight in being hidden in His story rather than fighting to be known to history.

We can stand in whatever place He has for us—safe, secure, and free in the innermost chamber of our hearts, minds, souls, and spirits.

In calm or chaos, visible or invisible, we can feel His gaze of delight upon us and feel our hearts begin to unfurl. We can become steady. We can be assured.

Friend, I'm a sucker for praying on the beach. In my twenty-five years of traveling the shore, I don't think a year has passed without walking the shoreline with a prayer or petition on my lips. And so, I'd like to close each chapter with a prayer—for you, for us.

Captain of my Soul,

You are the sustaining breath of my life; Your Spirit is the wind in my sails. I have believed this. Known this. Proclaimed this. I remember well the days of first-flush love, clinging to the promise that You Yourself are more than enough for me and seeking the kingdom first, leaving anything else squarely in Your nail-scarred hands.

I admit, here, that my heart is often infected by the world's ways of seeking meaning and significance. I have been more mindful of the economy of the culture than the affirmation of the King. The results have been frantic living, unceasing comparison, and insecurity. Though I can see the poor fruit, I often forget the root—the lie that whispers, "Human eyes, opinions, and acceptance are the source of significance."

But You are my first love, and there is nothing more significant in all of life than being a part of Your story. Help me see the beauty on the pages You write. Help me to unlearn and relearn the glorious hidden life of diving deep with You. Amen.

CHAPTER 2

Seen in the Storm

"Then I passed by and saw you."
Ezekiel 16:8 (bsb)

Depending on the sources you consult, the *junonia* is the gold standard of seashells. It is relatively small; the largest ever found is reported to be six inches long.[1] With a creamy husk and polka-dotted with a brown, leopard skin–like pattern, this seashell is eagerly hunted by beachcombers who flock to Sanibel Island, Florida[2]; even a small one can fetch a hefty sum. The familiar tongue twister "She sells seashells by the seashore" takes on a whole new meaning when the specimen in question is one of these rare beauties.

This same tenacious pursuit marks the hunt for the elusive Scotch bonnet, North Carolina's state shell. Recently, the largest one on record in North Carolina was found off the beaches of Ocracoke.[3] It was an unusual find on an unusual Outer Banks

21

island, which, for many years, boasted the country's smallest school-house[4] and still boasts wild horses that run the beach, descended from horses of ancient Spanish shipwrecks.

These unique sea jewels rarely make an appearance. One has to be looking for them constantly. Seashell hunters know to keep their eyes peeled—especially after storms, when the sea is most likely to give up its valuable oceanic treasures.

As we think about keeping our eyes peeled, let's visit another Concealed Charactmpture.

CONCEALED CHARACTERS

Hagar

No one kept an eye peeled for me as I traveled a road littered with as much sand as any shore.

I ran from what nipped at my heels and feasted on my heart. The desert silt mingled with my tears and coated my face, like the shame in which I had been born, the shame I knew I could never shake as easily as I shook out my sandals every night. I knew I would never come clean from it.

Escape—through death, dehydration, what have you—would be the likely endgame. But that something must change—this was never in doubt.

I hadn't asked for the life I'd been given. I had been born into it—from my first squalling breath to the night my master procured me in Egypt, to the giving of my body to that same master to produce an heir, to the mistreatment I had received at the hands of my mistress, Sarai—the one who had hatched the plan for the God-circumventing morass in the first place.

I had always been impoverished, but poverty of agency was worst of all. I had no choice in most things. But to escape and run—this I could choose. This I did choose.

Perhaps someone in the desert would see me and help me. Perhaps I would happen upon the kindness of some stranger who would help me homeward. Perhaps a thief would dispatch me from this life to the next.

Perhaps.[5]

God Moves First

Before we look at the component of this story that leaves me slack-jawed, we must first sit down with the fact that Hagar did not find God; God found Hagar. Let's look at her story:

> The angel of the LORD found her by a spring of water in the wilderness, the spring on the way to Shur. And he said, "Hagar, servant of Sarai, where have you come from and where are you going?" She said, "I am fleeing from my mistress Sarai." The angel of the LORD said to her, "Return to your mistress and submit to her." The angel of the LORD also said to her, "I will

surely multiply your offspring so that they cannot be numbered for multitude." . . .

So she called the name of the LORD who spoke to her, "You are a God of seeing," for she said, "Truly here I have seen him who looks after me." (Genesis 16:7–10, 13 ESV)

Notice the phrase "the angel of the LORD" in this account. When this phrase is used in the Bible, scholars tell us it is most likely a theophany. A *theophany* is a physical embodiment of God, most rigidly defined as occurring in the Old Testament. Scholars believe this is likely a human embodiment of God Himself: "On the run from her mistress, Hagar met the *angel of the Lord*, God in human form who most often appears in dire personal crises to bring assurance of salvation."[6] The angel of the Lord also made a glorious appearance in a wrestling match with Jacob (Genesis 32) and to Gideon (Judges 6), of whom we will speak later. Regardless of the intricacies and implications of Old Testament theophanies, what is astonishing is that they happen at all.[7]

Hagar wasn't looking for God when she ran away, but God was most certainly looking for her. And the Bible says God found her in a very specific place: by a spring in the wilderness, likely running back to Egypt.[8] When you are on the run for your life— emotionally, spiritually, psychologically, and physically—you still cannot outrun God. He runs to find you. It is amazing, I think, to see the radicalness of the gospel—"You did not choose me, but I chose you" (John 15:16); "This is love: not that we loved God, but that he loved us and sent his Son" (1 John 4:10)—reflected right here in the messy middle of Genesis.

God moves first.

God moves first.

Interlude

Selah.

I need to "selah" on that astonishing encounter for just a moment. *Selah* is a musical notation in the Psalms that means "interlude."[9] It's a pause in the music. During my seasons of storm, I need to curl myself inside a glorious pause, a transformative interlude.

Friend, maybe you know exactly what it's like to need a selah too. When the earth hurts and your own efforts fail and human intervention is waylaid, you flop your marooned heart and hopes beside a spring in the wilderness, hidden from everyone. Yet I want to encourage you: God has His eye on you—not to bruise your battered heart or to turn you inside out and critique you but to bring to you the only balm that can heal you. When you are experiencing spiritual heart failure, God will resuscitate you. Whenever you think you are alone, think again.

The world gives us plausible-sounding lies, which we load onto our spiritual backs and cart into our spiritual lives: *Move first. Be a mover and a shaker for what you believe in. If you don't post, does the moment even count? How else will you make an impact (and feel valuable)? Craft and curate your identity. It's all up to you.* Even as Christ chasers, we can be tempted to bear-hug falsity.

I often must minister Jesus' words back to my stubborn heart: "My Father is always at his work to this very day, and I too am working" (John 5:17).

Nothing stops His work. No difficulty impedes it. No lifelong bondage or brokenness slows it down. No human opinion shrinks it. Jesus is always working things out, making things beautiful, causing things to work together for our good, and making first moves (just as He did with the man crippled by the pool of Siloam).

The truth of the gospel is that we don't have to make the first

25

> God is coming to find us. God is coming to find you.

move. We are enjoined to simply respond to the grace that has been lavishly poured on our wandering, listless hearts—like the grace God poured on Hagar in her sandy, waterless wilderness.

God is coming to find us.

God is coming to find you.

Calling Names

Abraham. Sarah. Moses. Samuel. Elijah. Philip. Zacchaeus. Saul. Martha. Simon. Lazarus. Hagar.

When God calls a name in Scripture, it's a momentous occurrence; the list of people addressed by God or Jesus in Scripture is not lengthy. Sometimes when God calls someone's name, it is to arrest the person's attention. Sometimes it is for emphasis. Sometimes it differentiates the person called from others nearby.[10] Often, particularly in the Old Testament, it accompanies a great promise.[11]

This was the case with Hagar. After God spoke her name, acknowledged her difficult circumstance as an enslaved person, and told her the baby in her womb was a son, God moved next toward this earth-rending promise: "I will increase your descendants so much that they will be too numerous to count" (Genesis 16:10).

This flattens me.

Scholars say that this promise mirrors another covenant,[12] and the promise it mirrors is an audacious one: "[God] took [Abraham] outside and said, 'Look up at the sky and count the stars—if indeed you can count them. . . . So shall your offspring be'" (15:5). In fact, later we read it wasn't just Abraham whose descendants became twelve tribes; Ishmael also became the father of twelve tribes: "And as for Ishmael, I have heard you: I will surely bless him; I will make him fruitful and will greatly increase his numbers. He will be the father of twelve rulers, and I will make him into a great nation" (17:20).

We often focus so much on the enmity between Ishmael's offspring (those of Arabic descent) and Isaac's offspring (those of Jewish descent) that we hop, skip, and jump over God's promise to Hagar (and Hagar's offspring) altogether. A promise of generational blessing.[13] God promised to bless this heartbroken, terrified mother—an equivalent promise on the scale of God's promise to Abraham,[14] given to Hagar in the middle of an emotional sandstorm. All of that and more is contained in and follows the calling of Hagar's name.

What do we make of this divine speaking of a name when we feel invisible? Is there a hopeful nugget hidden in the sand? Simply, I believe it is this: your lack of visibility to humanity cannot determine your destiny. The truth of the matter is that your destiny does not spring from any human. Humanity cannot make, unmake, or negate it. The mouth of mankind cannot pronounce or renounce it. God alone is the arbiter of such things.

> **Your lack of visibility to humanity cannot determine your destiny.**

Holy Q&A

If the Lord calling Hagar by name and issuing her a generational promise has me slack-jawed, this next portion of Hagar's story has me reduced by the glory of it all.

I've always been fascinated with the questions of Scripture. For more than a decade, I've been diving into the interesting way God engages the hearts of His beloved creatures with holy interrogatives. Depending on which scholar you consult and how the original language is rendered, it is patently clear that Jesus asked hundreds of holy questions during His ministry on earth. He was constantly showing His engagement and drawing out the hearts of His listeners by asking them questions:

- When Jesus asked the woman for a drink of water in John 4:7, His question had a double meaning. He was thirsty from His tiring journey, *and* He knew He would be talking to the woman about her deep spiritual thirst, offering Himself as the only legitimate satiation. Physical water *and* spiritual water.
- In Matthew 16:15, Jesus asked His disciples, "But what about you? . . . Who do you say I am?" The Messiah knew exactly who He was, but He wanted to know if the disciples knew who He was.
- In Genesis 3:9, God called to Adam, "Where are you?" God didn't ask this question because He had misplaced Adam. God asked Adam this question because *Adam* had misplaced Adam. In answering God's question, Adam realized exactly where he happened to be: "I heard you in the garden, and I was afraid because I was naked; so I hid" (v. 10). *Afraid. Naked. Hiding.* (Caught in the embrace of an unholy triumvirate.)

Questions in the mouth of God both engage *and* reveal the heart.

And in Genesis 16, God asked two piercing queries of Hagar: "Hagar, slave of Sarai, *where have you come from,* and *where are you going?*" (v. 8).

Hagar answered, "I'm running away from my mistress Sarai" (v. 8). She was likely escaping to the only place she knew: home to Egypt.

I could weep at the tender wonder of that holy Q&A. God's questions somehow nestle beside my unspoken need. Maybe you feel it as well?

Friend, where have you come from? God wants to know. *How did you get here, today? What happened? What made you run? What evil uncoiled itself, slithered toward you, and then recoiled itself around your heart? What shame or lack of agency forced your hand? What messy moment unmade you and remade you hard as a stone? What threat, what bully, made you doubt any small strength you thought you had? What slow drip of doubt has reduced you to ash?*

Where have you come from? Take a moment—perhaps in the here and now—and write your answer in the margins of this book or speak it aloud to Jesus. Our hands can unburden our minds; our mouths can unburden our hearts. I believe Jesus wants to retrace every unexpected detour, waylay, brutality, confusion, and step—wrongly and rightly. He wants it all. And I think He is the only One who can handle the "all" of it. He truly wants to know where you are coming from.

Friend, where are you going?

It's not a scolding parent's voice that might sound like, *Where do you think you're going?* It's a gentle reach-out. An unfurled and welcoming hand. He finds us beside our desert springs when we're gutted from our forced fleeing and asks us, with all the love in the known universe, *Where are you going, My child?*

What caused you to think this brutal burning of the bridge is your only option? Why do you cut the anchor and set sail on a sea of tumult? Have you any map for what comes next? On what course would you like to set your ship?

The Holy Dialogue

In theatre, the two most common categories of speech are monologues and dialogues. *Mono* means one. *Logue* means speech or speaking. *One-speak.* A monologue happens when one character unpacks ideas and thoughts in a lengthy speech with no other character interjecting other words or thoughts midflow.

Very often, this is how God communicates with His beloved creations. God speaks; we listen. Think of God's answer at the end of the book of Job, when Yahweh (God) spoke without interruption for what we read as almost two full chapters (40:7–41:34). Job did not interject; he was stunned to silence. In fact, when Job finally replied at the end of Yahweh's majestic monologue, he said of his previous words questioning God, "Surely I spoke of things I did not understand, things too wonderful for me to know" (42:3).

Yet there are other unusual and stupefying instances when God allows dialogue—invites and initiates it, even—which is what we witness with Hagar in Genesis 16. The Maker of heaven and earth was communicating with a runaway nobody (Hagar's name means "flight"), and He was inviting her to dialogue with Him. *Two-speak.*

We cannot overstate this exchange or other exchanges in Scripture like it. Speaking of Yahweh's conversation with Abraham, Bible scholar Robert W. Jenson said, "Rather, somehow or other an actual conversation takes place . . . that will be characteristic of the relationship between God and the people of Israel throughout their entire history together. The God of Israel is a talkative one."[15] We serve a God who communicates. And this communicative act, among a million other things, is one of the things that sets our living God apart from other so-called gods.

Before we get to the radical act of Hagar *giving God a name*, let's emphasize, once again, the fact that God invited her into a *dialogue* with Him.

And this isn't the only time in Scripture we see Him (or His representative) draw women into conversation. We also see dialogue with Eve, Sarai, Martha, and the Samaritan woman at the well.[16] One conversation that has always fascinated me is when the angel Gabriel appeared to Mary and announced that she had been chosen to bear Emmanuel in her womb (Luke 1:26–38). The Messiah was coming, and she was the young mama-to-be who would carry Him. After the angel's announcement, she asked, "How will this be . . . since I am a virgin?" (v. 34). Her last bit of verbal communication with Gabriel was a yes and amen: "May it happen to me as you have said" (v. 38 CSB). *As You have spoken, God. As You have communicated. As You have said. You are a God who says. Let it be done to me.* Pretty astounding.

Where are you going?

Once, while caught in a teenage dramedy of my own making, I decided to run away from home. (Things like this were oddly sort of common in the 1980s, as were sneaking out and hitchhiking, but I digress.) I packed a duffel bag with pink foam rollers, unitards, leg warmers, and asymmetrical sweatshirts and slammed the door behind me with a house-rattling *thud*. I waited at the end of the street for a theatre friend to pick me up and spirit me away to my getaway—which happened to be her house. (I'm sure she called my parents as soon as we arrived to let them know their "runaway" was safe.) What I remember most about that day are long swims in a giant pond by her house and tête-à-têtes under a weeping willow. The details are quite lost to me now—I can't even recall what caused such a dramatic fight and flight from my home—but what is not lost is that my friend came to collect me, stayed alongside me, and conversed with me. After spending one night and the next day at Lauren's house, I was ready to return home. Lauren had helped me talk it out.

And God, in Hagar's difficult story, did the same. After hearing her plight, God delivered some very hard-to-swallow wisdom: "Go back to your mistress and submit to her" (Genesis 16:9). Now, this instruction to return to Sarah is very difficult for us as moderns to understand. While Scripture does not indicate that there was physical abuse in Hagar's story, there was certainly emotional and psychosocial mistreatment. Why in heavens would God tell her to return? We must remember that the societal system at that time was communal and familial. Safety and provision for women were within the familial structure. A woman was generally safe as part of a family group or tribe, but as an individual, she could be subject to the whims of a warlike culture.[17] Pregnant and alone, without the covering of a family system, Hagar would've surely been at risk in such a savage and unpredictable culture. With no family to care for her and her unborn child, she would have no protection from the warrior tribesmen who combed the surrounding areas. No covering. No sustenance. And so . . . God told her to return.

(As a sidenote, let's acknowledge that our modern culture is not Hagar's culture. Today, God provides refuge for abused women in a myriad of ways that *do not involve returning to their abusers.* Any woman who feels unsafe needs to hear that God's love is a rescuing love, and His heart for His beloved is healing and freedom.[18])

God not only pointed Hagar in the direction where she would receive care (culturally speaking) but also buoyed her heart with the knowledge that she carried a providential promise in her womb. Not only would Abraham's family line increase; hers would too. God said to Hagar, "Behold, you are pregnant and shall bear a son. You shall call his name Ishmael [which means 'God hears'], because *the LORD has listened* [heard with intention] to your affliction [depression, misery]" (v. 11 ESV).

Holy Hearing

The Lord has listened.

God has heard. God has responded.

One of the things that reinforces my faith whenever stormy winds prevail is that the Bible is too complex and messy to be falsely constructed. These are not fairy tales in which the marginalized woman bears the underdog son who will one day rise and be the king of the proverbial hill. God does not candy-coat the kind of person that this child, Ishmael, will be: Undisciplined. Antagonistic. Living in hostility toward his brothers (Genesis 16:12). Eventually, Hagar's story would also be used as an illustration of the law versus grace (Galatians 4:21–31).

The Lord told the truth to Hagar. This truth was unvarnished and perhaps unwanted, but even in the difficulty and the affliction, the promise of God's great reward to Hagar never wavered. Hagar and her descendants would not be reduced to dust; she would bear evidence that the fingerprints of the Holy One were all over her marginalized life.

God has heard. God has responded.

As we read in Scripture, Yahweh not only heard Hagar, but several chapters later, when Abraham painfully and predictably sent away an older Hagar and an older Ishmael in Genesis 21, Hagar had another awe-filled encounter with the Lord. This time, God responded not just to Hagar's cry but also the boy's.

> God heard the boy crying, and the angel of God called to Hagar from heaven and said to her, "What is the matter, Hagar? Do not be afraid; God has heard the boy crying as he lies there. Lift the boy up and take him by the hand, for I will make him into a great nation."
>
> Then God opened her eyes and she saw a well of water. So she went and filled the skin with water and gave the boy a drink. (Genesis 21:17–19)

The first time God found Hagar, He found her by a spring. During the second encounter, God directed her to a well.

During the first encounter, God heard the cries of the mother. During the second, He heard the cries of the son.

God was the first responder on each desperate scene—separated by years—reiterating His concern for their welfare and His promise that Ishmael's offspring would become a great nation.

God heard. God responded.

God Has Seen

All that was, is, and would be in Hagar's story caused this woman with no societal voice to use the voice she had to cry out to God, to name Him: "You are the God who sees me" (Genesis 16:13). In Hebrew, this name is *El Roi*; it's the only time in Scripture we see God so named.

"I have now seen the One who sees me," Hagar continued (v. 13). There is something here I previously missed in my years of teaching this particular story; I was so focused on the astonishing fact that God saw Hagar and that Hagar gave God a name that I underemphasized the first phrase of the above scripture.

I have now seen.

I. Have. Now. Seen.

How often in my thirty-plus years of walking with Jesus have my spiritual eyes been shut because of pain or spiritual amnesia or stubborn opposition? Why is it so easy for me to choose *not* to see? I don't want to be like the people Jeremiah warned, "who have eyes but do not see" (Jeremiah 5:21), yet far too often, I live just like that—like a child who will not look her father in the face for fear of what she might see there. In the next chapter, we will look at our very human propensity *not* to see and perhaps what can be done about it, but for now, I am asking God for a heart like Hagar's—who, with eyes full of fear, still looked straight at Almighty God.

Even in the deepest despair and desperation, I long for eyes to see, a heart to hear, and the brave audacity to name.

When my children were younger and beachcombed the Outer Banks, it always amazed me what amazed them. Their treasures had an . . . interesting quality to them. Their stubby-fingered palms cradled curlicue casings from some molting creature, the half mask of a crab's hard shell, a pocked lure (sans hook, of course), or a stick. In their cupped hands, the detritus of the deep was transformed into the wonders of the waves. The assessment all turned on who was doing the beholding. Their affection, their delight, endowed those ordinary objects with meaning, merit, legitimacy, value, and worth.

The divine narrative of our lives is not, ultimately, ours to compose. It is His.

The same is true of us. Dinged up on our worst days; delightful on our best. Remembered by some; forgotten by all.

No matter how we fill in the blanks of our burdens, we must allow a greater language to speak over us. The divine narrative of our lives is not, ultimately, ours to compose. It is His. No matter how the chapters of our stories turn and twist, no matter how the details play out, Hagar's assessment of God was true: *You are the God who sees me. I have now seen the One who sees me.*

It is in His sight that we are rescued, redirected, and resurrected.

I pray that we all may learn to gaze back into this heavenly view.

El Roi,

Invisibility cuts deep, Lord. To be unseen. Unnoticed. Or noticed, then dismissed. Oh, how it hurts and prompts thoughts I would never say aloud. Do the things I do matter . . . do my thoughts matter . . . do I matter? To You, I pour out this lament of soul and listen for Your answer.

Help me reject the lie and run after the Truth: I am made in Your own image. Your precious life's blood was poured out for me. You invite me to join in the work You are doing. You love me. And You alone define me.

Help me receive the truth that mattering to You is the highest honor, the deepest safety. Keep me from entrusting my heart to the things of this world. I want to choose what nourishes the truth rather than what decays. Help me to tilt my chin and catch a glimpse of You, the One Who Sees, and the One who has said, "I will counsel you with my loving eye on you" (Psalm 32:8). I trust You with my frail heart. I know You will see to it. Amen.

CHAPTER 3

Invisible Glory

The Son is the image of the invisible God.
COLOSSIANS 1:15

In the Outer Banks, there's a phrase you hear as consistently as the undulating flow of the Atlantic waves: *The Lost Colony*. The stories run the gamut from hazy history to technicolor entertainment. *The Lost Colony* is the title of the country's longest-running outdoor symphonic drama,[1] performed in the Outer Banks town of Manteo, which was Andy Griffith's home in his later years.

Countless books and documentaries have been devoted to sleuthing out the mystery of the Lost Colony of Roanoke, which was the first English settlement on the continent, predating the Jamestown settlement by twenty years. When supplies ran desperately low, the governor of the colony set sail for England, and, after almost three years of delay, he finally returned to find . . . nothing and no one. The entire colony—including his daughter and grand-daughter (the first English child born in the New World)—had disappeared into the mists of the Outer Banks.

While touring the eerily empty settlement, the governor found two carved messages on a tree and a post, respectively: *CRO* and *CROATOAN*, which many believed meant the colony had relocated to Croatoan Island, modern-day Hatteras Island, led by the Native American people group, the Croatoans. But when the governor sailed south to reach the island, his vessel was buffeted by terrible weather, and the ship had to turn back. Without breaching the shores of Croatoan Island to form a search party, no one could ever say for sure what happened to the members of the Roanoke colony. It has remained an enduring mystery ever since.

For four centuries, various theories have persisted. Some believe the colonists were lost in the Great Dismal Swamp as they moved north. Others believe the colony was wiped out by a hurricane. Still others persist in believing that the colonists, helped by Native Americans, relocated somewhere in the area.

Recently, there have been some exciting developments regarding the whereabouts of the Lost Colony, which I've been watching like a farmer spying for the first head of wheat. It's quite possible that the Lost Colony is not lost at all but actually hidden in plain sight.[2]

Common Chorus

Sometimes that is exactly how I feel.

I could regale you with stories of times I felt hidden in plain sight—videos where my name was altogether wrong, dressing rooms with someone else's name pasted upon them. In conversations I was often referred to as "the tall girl" or "the understudy" (which I was for two years on Broadway). Once, in a ministry setting, at a time when I had taken over for a well-respected minister, a woman in the audience yelled that she missed the other minister by name just as I was getting ready to take the stage.

Now, this is no woe-is-me workshop. Promise. I'm acutely aware of the overflowing cup of my life, and I've experienced unmitigated joy at joining Jesus in the adventure of faith. His presence is my life's highest peak. Yet I've also had an odd string of invisibility running through my life's tapestry, right alongside opportunities that were very visible.

Seen and unseen by people, often at the same time.

I hesitated in sharing this tender chapter in my story, but I think many of us are members of the same chorus, part of a common symphony. Often when I hear someone reveal a thorn in their personal narrative, I exhale internally, thinking, *I'm not the only one. I'm so with you on that.* Vulnerability can be redemptive because, whether or not our experiences have challenged our visibility and validity in the same way, most of us have had moments that left us sucking wind emotionally, pondering in the dark watches of the night, *Does anything really matter? Do I matter?*

Likely, we've all had moments where we're seen physically yet still feel invisible or invalidated in some way.

In Colossae's Sites

There is a certain biblical city that lies unseen, hidden in plain sight. Disguised as an otherworldly berm in southern Turkey, the remains of Colossae are buried underground. However, Colossae, which was devastated by an earthquake in the first century, is beginning to come back to life as an archaeological dig is getting underway.[3] In my fantasies I am there, moving dirt, dusting artifacts, and celebrating when evidence of the Colossian believers' community finally sees the light of day.

Before we put our scriptural Hope Diamond under the microscope, I would like to invite you down a sandy road, over two thousand years ago, to an outpost called Colossae. When consulting scholars and commentators, certain adjectives make the rounds like a pop song's hook about this particular throwaway town: *unimportant, small, hidden, obscure*.[4] You get the snapshot, I think.

This city was hidden from the grit and grind of Ephesus and the palpable energy of Galatia's power grid. Think of the unincorporated municipalities that dot the outskirts of any major city. By the time Paul composed (or Paul's scribe took dictation of) the letter we know in our Bibles as the book of Colossians, Colossae was decidedly unimportant. In fact, it was one of the few places receiving a letter that Paul himself never visited.[5]

Many scholars believe the Colossian church was likely started by Epaphras, Paul's student, as a response to the incredible ministry that was happening in Ephesus during the two years Paul taught in the school of Tyrannus there.[6] Think of a large university's satellite schools, and you'll get the idea. The movement of God mushroomed more than one hundred miles away in little ol' hidden Colossae.

Paul wrote to the Colossian believers while imprisoned in Rome, and he encouraged the congregation to see the all-encompassing goodness and glory of God as revealed through Christ Jesus.[7] He told his cherished fellow sojourners,

We always thank God, the Father of our Lord Jesus Christ, when we pray for you, because we have heard of your faith in Christ Jesus and of the love you have for all God's people— the faith and love that spring from the hope stored up for you in heaven and about which you have already heard in the true message of the gospel that has come to you. (Colossians 1:3–6)

The letter continues with language loftier than a Shakespearean soliloquy. And since my favorite roles have been of the Shakespearean ilk, I am a sucker for a lofty soliloquy. Look at some of Paul's soaring phraseology:

The Son is the image of the invisible God, the firstborn over all creation. For in him all things were created: things in heaven and on earth, visible and invisible, whether thrones or powers or rulers or authorities; all things have been created through him and for him. He is before all things, and in him all things hold together. (vv. 15–17)

In Him everything is held together, including . . . well, everything: world systems, the powers that be, and the uncertainties that threaten to undo us—whether it's medical bills we can't pay or the chaos of a move. Betrayal by friends or the badgering of the Enemy. No matter what shoves us off-balance, Jesus is the axis of the spinning earth and our spinning hearts. A truth this encompassing will lash a wild soul to a sturdy mast. Jesus, the Above All, is the All in All.

The book of Colossians is an achingly beautiful invitation to affirm Jesus' supremacy and to saturate ourselves in the undiluted gospel. On the whole, Colossians is an opus for the hopeless.

And yet, there was something else at work in the midst of the Colossian believers' household of faith—a spiritual *shenaniganizing* that threatened to bloom like dangerous red algae, spreading throughout the congregation.

Several years ago, my family went on vacation in Seaside, Florida. If you've seen the 1998 movie *The Truman Show*, most of that bucolic film was captured there. Seaside feels more perfect than a place has a right to be. On the first day we were set to head to the beach, we learned that an aggressive algae bloom had also come to town. My husband and I chanced the waters, as the surface looked so lovely. In short order, my legs were intertwined with the seagrass, and, as we exited the ocean, we coughed and struggled to breathe. The algae symptoms caught us off guard. Later, we learned that when red algae, or red tide, is in the water, it consumes more than its fair share of oxygen, leaving living beings coughing and struggling for air.[8]

I sometimes wonder how the "red tide" of the false doctrine that crept into the church at Colossae might have affected the body. Here, I wonder about the response of another Concealed Character—a woman named Apphia. She is listed in the greeting of Paul's letter to Philemon (v. 2) and recognized as one of the Colossian Christians who hosted a house church. One commentator noted she was "not improbably the wife of Philemon."[9]

CONCEALED CHARACTERS
Apphia

But what are we to make of it, Philemon? Perhaps to refuse to quench the flame is to fan it. Without daylight, mold spreads among the grain. None of us wishes to see the unalloyed work of Jesus defiled; what has dross to do with gold? My mind is eaten up with concern.

Ariadne said our bodies should be harshly, even brutally, disciplined, and that angels themselves had been part of the great resurrection, so perhaps they deserve greater acclaim—worship, even. She whispered that many older people among us had passed on to them the strange mystery and logic.

Philemon, how can this be the undiluted gospel of Jesus? It is not in keeping with all we have learned. How do we straighten this wily thread in the fabric? How do we unwind it without undoing the entire tapestry? Most among us do not sing this strange new song, yet it only takes a loud off-key voice to mar a unified chorus.

I speak out my worries to Jesus in prayer, and He assures me He will be faithful to help. It has been moons since we dispatched to Rome to ask Paul's guidance. My mind is consumed with concern for him; sleep is a wisp I cannot catch. Will Rome imprison all who claim the name? Will we all suffer such chains? When I feel brave, I whisper in the watches of the night: "If it is so, then let it be so."

We must pray that the flock's faith may not fail. We must petition for Paul daily, asking God to strengthen him, bound as he is, as many have been so strengthened. I pray that Paul's answer will come tomorrow, or the day after that, and that there will be enough sunshine in the apostle's words to expose the enemy phantom in the Enemy's shadows.

The Colossian Controversy

It's hard to give a perfectly pristine definition of the problem Paul alluded to in his letter to this congregation. Scholars simply refer to it as the "Colossian controversy" or the "Colossian heresy," as it involved multiple factors and complexities. Suffice it to say that some in the Colossian church had fallen prey to a monster—a spiritual Frankenstein, if you will—blending law-based rule keeping with ecstatic angel worship. These elements were melded with the legitimate worship and understanding of Jesus and the gospel. Paul warned these believers: "See to it that no one takes you captive through hollow and deceptive philosophy, which depends on human tradition and the elemental spiritual forces of this world rather than on Christ" (Colossians 2:8). Though there are differing opinions about what the Colossian controversy was, there is no doubt this strange new teaching was counterfeit, held no weight, and was poised to deceive.[10]

The kind of blending we see in Colossae is referred to as *syncretism*, which is when two dissimilar things are combined until something new is created. Think of a spiritual Chimera, a mythological creature made up of disparate parts: a lion's head, a goat's body, and a serpent's tail. When syncretism rears its ugly head in Christianity, it functions a bit like cooking an unholy meal in a spiritual Crock-Pot—throw a little pickle juice, duck, and peanut butter in that melding machine and hope that somehow, something tasty might be achieved.

When Jonathan and I were newly married, I thought I'd try my boldest Julia Child by adding an *entire* can of orange juice concentrate to a chicken à l'orange dish. Surely if the recipe asked for a bit of an orange peel, an entire undiluted can would be even better, right? Needless to say, the meal was a foodie flop; Jonathan could stomach only one bite. Those ingredients didn't play well together, and they couldn't produce a satisfying meal.

Though a pale metaphor, this mix gives an image of the misled spiritual chefs' creation in Colossae. They wanted something more than Jesus when what they really needed was more *of* Jesus.

Minding the Mix

There are times I have secretly wanted more than Jesus. And there are places and times I have not minded my mix, particularly as it relates to my identity, value, and worth. As someone who has walked with Jesus for decades, I know *to the marrow* that Jesus is my life's bones, my heart's beat, and my hope's iron. I have eaten this, breathed this, and known this. And yet, when circumstances leave me questioning whether I matter, I find myself standing over my spiritual Crock-Pot, adding dashes of the world, pinches of illegitimate visibility, and dollops of social media. I find myself striving to be seen by human eyes, hoping for the hit of their admiration.

How about you, friend? Is there a way you are tempted to add something to Jesus? Maybe it is something that even sounds good or spiritual, like, *If I pray enough, nothing bad will befall me. If I serve Jesus faithfully, He will make sure I'm given "more" for His glory. If I give, I'll never have financial need. If I perfectly keep the rules, I'll be more acceptable to Him.* Is there anywhere you're not minding your mix?

When I find myself in these places, I realize I'm being tempted to ingest a dastardly meal: it's still mostly Jesus, but it's not only Jesus. At those times, I have served up my unholy mix.

Likewise, the Colossians were not minding their mix, adding elements of ecstatic angel worship with rule keeping and harsh treatment of the body (asceticism). That's why Paul urged them:

> Do not let anyone judge you by what you eat or drink, or with regard to a religious festival, a New Moon celebration or a Sabbath day. These are a shadow of the things that were to come; the reality, however, is found in Christ. Do not let anyone who delights in false humility and the worship of angels disqualify you. Such a person also goes into great detail about what they have seen; they are puffed up with idle notions by their unspiritual mind. They have lost connection with the head, from whom the whole body, supported and held together by its ligaments and sinews, grows as God causes it to grow. (2:16–19)

What was happening among the Colossae household of faith was a bit too early for the onset of Gnosticism, a set of beliefs that only the supposed elite were given to understand. (Think of Gnosticism as secret handshakes to get into a swanky, members-only club.) Yet some thinkers believe it's possible that the seeds of what would become Gnosticism were being sown in that particular congregation.[11] Whatever the case, there were some spiritual beliefs and practices in which some Colossians were trusting that were, at best, a bad kettle of fish and, at worst, a spiritual *Titanic* about to collide with an iceberg.

Paul used many of the phrases from this Colossian controversy that was tempting new believers to "hide" themselves in counterfeit beliefs and practices, and he turned those false phrases on their heads, pointing to why Jesus is preeminent above any human secret or gnostic-like doctrine. He wrote to (and of) these believers, "My goal is that they may be encouraged in heart and united in love, so that they may have the full riches of complete understanding, in order that they may know the mystery of God, namely, Christ, in whom are hidden all the treasures of wisdom and knowledge" (2:2–3).

Paul turned these shipwrecking beliefs upside down and then right side up again with these words: "I have become [the church's] servant by the commission God gave me to present to you the word of God in its fullness—the mystery that has been kept hidden for ages and generations, but is now disclosed to the Lord's people" (1:25–26). In other words, there is no secret, hidden knowledge or secret, hidden way of worshiping God reserved for special people here on earth. Paul exclaimed there is nothing greater to be understood and lived than the mystery that has been revealed finally and fully, *through* and *in* Jesus.

Just a few paragraphs later, Paul penned the words that have become my often-wayward heart's North Star. Maybe these verses can help us all navigate home:

> Set your minds on things above, not on earthly things. For you died, and your life is now hidden with Christ in God. When

Christ, who is your life, appears, then you also will appear with him in glory. (3:2–4)

Figures of Life

I am an admitted word nerd; I blame the theatre for my propensity toward archaic words. One of my first tasks when working on a classical script was defining any unknown verbiage. I've never escaped my love of etymology (the development and "roots" of words), believing in some way that the root determines the fruit. So, if you would humor me, I'd like to look at three "figures" of speech in Colossians 3:2–3 that have become for me, over the course of writing this book, figures of life, which we will talk about in ascending order of pertinence for our time walking the spiritual beach together.

- The phrase: *set your minds*
- The preposition: *with*
- The adjective: *hidden*

The Phrase

"Set your minds" is such a life-giving antidote for the tendency to wander toward the world in our thinking. This Greek phrase, *phroneo*, can mean "to have an attitude, to ponder, to honor, and to hold a view."[12]

For days and weeks, this is what I did with my black whelk. I held it in my view, rotating it from one angle to the next. That gives us a sampling of Paul's sense when he wrote, "Set your minds" (3:2). What we behold, in some ways, we become.

I can only imagine how relieved Apphia and Philemon would've been when Paul's letter finally reached them. Among other things, Paul told the Colossians to mull the truth over and over again like the waves falling upon the shore.

> **What we behold, in some ways, we become.**

But it is the additional understanding of "set your minds"—"to hold a view"[13]—that knocks me squarely back into one precipitous portion of my college dance class: the dreaded pirouette intensives. *Pirouette* is a French word meaning "to turn or to spin." And among the many mechanics of pirouetting, one was near impossible for me to master: spotting. Think of it this way: when a body is attempting to turn once, twice, or even three times around the fixed point of a leg at a high rate of speed, balance becomes a beast. To balance well, you must focus your eyes clearly on a fixed spot, no matter how fast the turn is. The way a dancer (or ice skater or gymnast) is trained to maintain balance is by singling out one spot on the wall (doorjamb, fire alarm, what have you) and focusing on that spot while everything is spinning. When you watch great dancers, look for their spotting technique—notice how their eyes hit an imperceptible spot every time they turn. They hold their predetermined view for a very short, almost undetectable amount of time, but it is this skill that helps them stay balanced, knowing right from left, up from down.

Some determined dance instructors helped me learn to spot by calling, "Allison, where's your spot?" each time I turned past whatever spot I had chosen without actually looking at it. They were teaching me to "hold the view." They also taught me to set my spot slightly higher than my eyeline, which kept my posture lifted and spinning, not lowered and collapsing. Without a proper spot, my center would not hold. Without focusing on Jesus, the spiritual center will not hold either.

Even after walking with Jesus for years, I need to circle back around to these foundational lessons. I am asking Jesus to help me to hold the view of a gospel-centered spot.

The Preposition

In Colossians 3:3, Paul continued, "Your life is now hidden *with* Christ in God."

A preposition is powerful, and it is no less so in Paul's letter. Simply put, a preposition is a part of speech that connects with another word and expresses its relationship with said word. Prepositions form bonds or links between words.

The phrase "*with* Christ" in verse 3 arrests my attention because it is somewhat unique in Paul's letters. Often we see the phrase "*in* Christ"—a phrase that appears 172 times in Scripture,[14] 97 of those times from the mind and pen of Paul.[15] But here Paul chose the preposition *with*, which means possessing a close connection and is a marker of association.[16] I believe no choice of words in Scripture is willy-nilly, as all of it is God-breathed (2 Timothy 3:16), so Paul's specific choice of preposition here piques my interest.

We see the same English preposition when Lazarus sat *with* Jesus at the table in Bethany (John 12:2) and when Jesus told His disciples He wouldn't drink the fruit on the vine until He drank it *with* them in His Father's kingdom (Matthew 26:29). Though there are more, both of these "withs" occur at a table, during a meal. There were few occurrences more tender in the first century than what occurred at a table. *Smith's Bible Dictionary* describes the close communion in this way: "In the time of the Savior, reclining was the universal custom. As several guests reclined on the same couch, each over-lapped with his neighbor . . . and rested his head on or near the breast of the One who lay behind him, he was then said to 'lean upon the bosom' of his neighbor."[17]

This bodily intimacy makes me lean into the phrase "*with* Christ" in Colossians 3:3 with a desire to lean on Jesus' chest at the table. I think of Him preparing to suffer, to bear the weight of the world, to become the sin of the world on the cross, and, still, to invite His disciples into the severe and necessary mercy of His pain. His proximity to His followers causes me to exhale with wonder. Because of what He has done, by faith, I am *with* Him; and because I am with Him, I am *in* Him.

As tender as the sense of "with" can be, it is also a preposition of power. Back in the 1990s, before electronic apps could schedule reservations, the attendant at the door decided who got in or who stayed out, especially if there was a boatload of folks coming and going. Often the keeper of the door (a.k.a. the bouncer/maître d'/ host) would ask, "Who are you with?" And then the pages would flip until the name of the person of merit was spotted, allowing us unknowns quick entry. I have many memories of trepidatious moments when the pages would fly, and I held my breath as I waited to discover whether I'd been remembered. During my years in Manhattan, knowing the name I was associated with was the key to unlocking the door and granting entry.

The Adjective

In Colossians 3:3, Paul used the adjective *hidden*: "Your life is now *hidden* with Christ."

The Greek word translated as "hidden" here is *krupto*, meaning to hide or, interestingly, to bury below, made invisible or hidden for safekeeping.[18] My mom had a habit of hiding important documents and money behind the slide-out portion of table picture frames. Back in the 1970s and '80s, home safes weren't all the rage yet, so important documents were stored in bank lockboxes or beneath mattresses. Mom wanted these important elements in close proximity to her, behind pictures of those dearest to her. After she died from a brutally quick bout of pancreatic cancer at age sixty-four, I remember discovering these hidden treasures, and they brought my relationship with her back to me for just a moment.

Hidden treasures in plain sight.

Because of our relationship with Jesus and His sacrifice on the cross, we are hidden, or buried, with Christ in God. Justice was poured on Him that grace might pour from Him. Because He so loved us and gave Himself for us, dying our death, we exchange our deserved death for His undeserved one; and in His death and resurrection, we die and rise. We now stand hidden behind the legs of Jesus, like a beloved child. His life and death—and our faith in them—unlock proximity and security in God that are impossible without them. We are united with Christ, hidden in heavenly places. We're already there, with Him, and our truest life—or *zoe*, in Greek—is Him. He is our everything. Our only. Our preeminent.

Paul continued by tipping his apostolic hat to the parousia, which is a fancy word that means the second coming of Christ, writing, "When Christ, who is your life, appears, then you also will appear with him in glory" (v. 4). Jesus—and all He is—is our very life, rather than some strange, syncretistic, Frankenstein-esque system of belief.

When I feel invisible or bereft or lacking, I remind my amnestic heart that I am hidden in the One in whom all spiritual treasures are hidden (2:3). And this truth settles the churning sea within. We don't have to hunt for the world's ways of mattering any longer. Why desire the created over the Creator? We can exit the ring; we can tap out of the illegitimate match of weighing our value by the wins, the belts, the prize money, the fame. We can live generously, toward others and ourselves, escaping the comparison trap and galloping free.

The heart of the matter is that I might always be lacking according to the calculus of the world, but in Christ, I lack no good thing (Psalm 34:10). All the mysteries of the ages—the full depths of which I could never plumb—are revealed in Jesus (Colossians 1:26), and through faith, I am hidden with Him in God (3:3).

This truth is hidden in plain sight. Herein lies the *great hope* of the gospel: the people of God, made in the image of God, are brought back to the heart of God through the Son of God.

> Herein lies the *great hope* of the gospel: the people of God, made in the image of God, are brought back to the heart of God through the Son of God.

Lost and Found

Speaking of being hidden in plain sight, it is becoming more and more possible—although archaeology is an ever-evolving field—that most of the Lost Colony members wound up on Croatoan

> **Oftentimes, the things we are looking for are hidden in plain sight.**

Island, exactly as they carved into the post and the tree more than four centuries ago. To date, a new dig on this island has uncovered thousands of artifacts that look very much like a significant settlement from the right era and of the right size was located there.[19] It seems that one of the most obvious answers for the Roanoke Colony's location was overlooked and underappreciated until recently.

Even if Hatteras Island isn't the final resting place of the Lost Colony, we know the evidence of the Lost Colony's final landing place isn't lost. Not really. It's out there somewhere, its roots still buried in the Outer Banks sand.

Oftentimes, the things we are looking for are hidden in plain sight.[20] Like Jesus.

Jesus,

    Today, I approach You with hope.

    Today, I ask You to clear my eyes.

    Today, I want to look outside myself and look up to You.

    Today, I ask, What is there to see?

    Give me the strength to notice the things You are doing, the places you are leading me. Steer my focus away from my circumstances and my concerns. My. My. My. Obsession with self binds. Obsession with You liberates. How many of my emotional tangles would be undone simply by looking at the only One who can unwind the mess? Press this truth into my heart, Alpha and Omega.

    Jesus, I grow ever more aware of this one unique life. This one time around the earth I have been given. I don't want to waste it searching for things that, at the end, will be nothing more than wisps in the wind. I want to seek the Son and not shadow.

    Today, these things I ask.

    Today, I trust.

    Amen and amen.

CHAPTER 4

Overlooked Gems

I have hidden your word in my heart.

PSALM 119:11

On a rainy day like only the Outer Banks can provide, I went to the aquarium, along with everyone else in the area. While in a little hallway, I saw an unusual photo of Outer Banks history—a line of men dressed in uniform, headed by Richard Etheridge, keeper of the Pea Island Lifesaving Station. The photo was more than a century old. Mr. Etheridge was a freedman—a formerly enslaved person who served with the Union in the Civil War. Mr. Etheridge was the first African American to hold such a post at a lifesaving station (picture a Coast Guard outpost before the Coast Guard existed). He and his crew often rescued those who shipwrecked in the Graveyard of the Atlantic, another ominous name for the Outer Banks. (The shoals and sandbars sometimes move so indiscriminately and violently that, before radar, storms could be world-enders, and navigation was a form of rolling the dice.)

After being intrigued by the photo in the hallway, I learned one particularly mouth-shutting story: In 1896, the *E. S. Newman* went down in a hurricane. Etheridge and his crew attempted to launch boats to make a rescue. The waves were too overwhelming for any rescue craft to maneuver, so the team went bodily into the churning water—nine times—throwing a line into the grounded ship and ultimately rescuing every person on board.

Until that rainy day, I had never even heard of Richard Etheridge and his courageous company. Pockets of people are learning of the heroic work they did (someone please make a movie) while facing repugnant racism, arson, and robbery.

As I think about history's oversight, I'm a pinch pained by their invisibility. Yet I wonder: Had they been any more visible during that dangerous age, would their work have even been possible? Maybe the Pea Island Lifesavers preferred obscurity, so they could do their work in peace without fear of retribution. Hard to say for certain, but we do know that Etheridge and his lifesaving crew pioneered an astonishing work on an Outer Banks island while being overlooked, the lasting effects of which we are only just beginning to understand.[1]

Excellence doesn't always equal exposure.

Turns out, excellence doesn't always equal exposure.

On and *For* Purpose

For years I've been gabbing about God's penchant for hiding His people purposefully now for a purpose much later. Hidden *on* purpose, *for* purpose, purposefully. A sovereign secreting away. We see a repeating pattern of long seasons of concealment in the lives of Joseph, Moses, David, Paul, and, of course, Jesus. When I see a scriptural pattern on repeat, I know to keep my eyes peeled. And when I personally chafe during seasons of concealment (which I often do), I peek into the spiritual rearview mirror, remember I am not alone, and head out on a spiritual treasure hunt.

The following spiritual presents were tucked away on the spiritual shelf for a mighty long while:

- Joseph: 11–13 years
- Moses: 30–40 years
- David: 15 years
- Paul: 2–3 years[2]
- Jesus: 30 years

Now, what the Lord was accomplishing during each of those concealed seasons was unique, and we could never fully explore their stories in this book. But we can rest assured that each season of hidden development was commissioned and utilized by a sovereign God.

Moses

After Moses fled Egypt and Egyptian law, he spent almost forty years in the deserts of Midian, learning to tend sheep in hidden hollows and valleys. Then the Lord called him from an unconsumed, fiery bush, choosing a stuttering voice to be His personal mouthpiece. Why did Moses have such a long hidden season? Even though Hebrews clearly states that Moses did not fear Pharaoh and chose to be identified and mistreated along with God's people, I've always wondered if, along with all that faith, there was some deep internal tempering still needed. Maybe Moses, who was a hothead extraordinaire, required some desert years to get some of Egypt's ways of mattering (entitlement, power, position) burned out of him. Pharaoh's palace would have afforded Moses every whimsy his heart could've ever imagined—nothing like a forty-year desert sojourn to reorient a heart.

Moses moved from hubris to deeper humility, and there's nothing like being a "hireling shepherd . . . of another man," as *The Pulpit Commentary* so aptly puts it, to help along said motion.[3] And even though Moses' actions reveal a "positive concern for the weak and oppressed, Moses did not yet qualify for the role of National Deliverer. Rather he was forced to abandon membership of the Egyptian royal court, and become an alien in a foreign land," T. D. Alexander wrote.[4]

On a much smaller scale, in my own life, the quiet, concealed years have the effect of washing off my false modes of being and counterfeit ways of coping, reducing me to the essentials of who I actually am. I'm just so darned good at adding superfluous emotional and social layers that can obscure the unique version of the imago Dei God created in me. I think most of us can slip into disguising ourselves. And so, mercifully, God brings us hidden years that cause a necessary stripping away—a loss of what cannot remain for a gain that cannot be lost.

I think of Paul calling to us across the ages, "I consider everything a loss because of the surpassing worth of knowing Christ Jesus my Lord" (Philippians 3:8). The writer of Hebrews said Moses "persevered because he saw him who is invisible" (11:27). Whether this is a reference to Moses' specific experience on Mount Sinai where he saw the back of the invisible God from his hiding place in the cleft of the rock (Exodus 33:22–23)[5] or an expression of his overall faith[6] (which would surely go along with Hebrews 11), I cannot help but be reminded of Colossians 3: the scripture that calls us to fix our minds and hearts on an invisible reality that is more real than the earth we run on and the seas in which we swim. During his years of hiddenness, Moses learned to trust in the Hidden One. Like Hagar before him, Moses saw Him who is invisible.

Yet, before Moses received the call from the unconsumed bush or heard the voice calling, "Let my people go" (Exodus 5:1), I wonder about the shell of a man Zipporah must have first encountered. Zipporah met Moses after he had fled the palace as a fugitive and rescued the daughters of the priest Jethro (Reuel) from unruly and thirsty shepherds by a well.

Here, I imagine Zipporah's conversation with one of her six sisters about the odd man they met (and left) by a desert well, much to the chagrin of their father.

CONCEALED CHARACTERS

Zipporah

Beulah, Father rants that we should have brought the man soaked in the scent of Egypt back to our tents. He said a rescuer had been sent to us at the well, and we did not esteem him. Did you not see Father just now complaining that he must make a double offering for our noxious oversight? He says that for us not to offer hospitality to such a defender will surely bring offense upon our heads. His hot breath cursing us "seven silly daughters" wears me to a sanded stone. Father continually asks after the man from Egypt; I've been told they are gone to seek him out in the desert. And in the meantime, Father goes on; I can see him wringing his hands in prayer to the gods that, finally, finally, one of his daughters might be moved from his tents to another man's. Always such questions: "Did you fancy him, Zipporah?" No. "Was he helpful, Zipporah?" Yes. "Was he strong, Zipporah?" Yes. "Was he handsome?" Somewhat.

Beulah, what I shall never speak out to our father is that the man was haunted, like the phantoms that stalk our world during the harvest, devouring the good and leaving the bad. A man such as this will never be domesticated again. He was a feral ghost. Gaunt and gutted. Hunted. One with his back to the rock because his secrets have sprung up as enemies. He is cornered once and for all.

Remember how he would only nod when we tried to speak to him, to ask after his people, that he spoke not a word, that he did not seem to understand us? When you commented on his form, he caught my eye. He shoved down a smirk. It was but a wisp, but it was recognition. He understands more than he pretends. This man, if they can even find him and return with him, is a marked man. Marked by whichever god he serves. Mark my words.[7]

Scripture tells us that Moses was found, came to dinner, and soon married Zipporah, the daughter of the Midianite priest Jethro. The Midianites were enemies of God's people, and they were regularly in conflict with them. They were one of the people groups involved in the selling and trafficking of Joseph (Genesis 37:36). In fact, they were the oppressors in a story we will look at soon—that of Gideon. To be sure, the Midianites were a motley assortment of characters.[8]

Zipporah, a Midianite, became the mother of Moses' sons Gershom and Eliezer, and she went on to play a starring role in a somewhat disquieting story in Exodus, in which she personally intervened between God's fury and her husband, Moses, completing the required circumcision of her son. T. D. Alexander wrote, "The unusual incident probably centers on Moses' continued lack of faith regarding his mission. Although God had assured him that he would deliver the Israelites out of Egypt because of his covenant with Abraham. Moses had failed to circumcise his own son as required by God under that very covenant."[9] This covenantal circumcision was an act that Moses, as the father, should've completed himself; Zipporah stepped in and completed what was lacking in Moses' obedience. Scripture says God was intent on snuffing out Moses altogether for this lapse of obedience; yet, because of Zipporah's audacity and bold agency, God relented.

I have to sit with the power of this Concealed Character, one who has much to teach my heart. A woman who stepped from the edges of the story, saving the life of her husband, the prophet of deliverance. After this odd chapter, Zipporah fades into the background of the Exodus story. At some point, Moses sent Zipporah away, and he reunited with her (and their two sons) years later while she was traveling with her father, Jethro. This Concealed

Character played an outsized, and maybe underappreciated, role in saving Moses' life while he was in a season of hidden waiting prior to the great exodus of God's people.

Jesus

After His miraculous birth announcement and narrative, His flight into Egypt to escape Herod, and His encounter with His parents at the temple when He was twelve, Jesus did not appear on the ministerial scene again until the miracle at the wedding of Cana. That's a long period of concealment.

As we read the accounts of Jesus' life in the Gospels, we see Him in seasons of concealed invisibility as well. After He began His ministry at His baptism, He endured a hidden desert battle for forty days and nights just before He pronounced Himself as the fulfillment of Isaiah's prophecy (Luke 4:21). He withdrew to pray all night long before choosing His disciples (Luke 6:12). He went by boat to a solitary place after He learned of His cousin John the Baptist's beheading (Matthew 14:13). And in His hour of agony, in the pressing place of Gethsemane, He moved to a solitary place to speak His agony into His Father's ears (Luke 22:41).

Privacy. Solitude. Withdrawal.

Even in His very public ministry, Jesus practiced the discipline of hiddenness by often forsaking the crowds for hidden fellowship with His Father (Luke 5:16). In one intriguing moment, Jesus praised His Father for hiding the truth of His messiahship to those who counted themselves as wise in their own eyes and revealing it to those who were simple, believing, and childlike. Jesus said, "I praise you, Father, Lord of heaven and earth, because you have hidden these things from the wise and learned, and revealed them to little children" (Matthew 11:25).

Again, we see that God reveals Himself as He wills, when He wills, and He seems to take special delight in revealing Himself to those who have little merit or power according to the world's litmus tests. As Paul said, "Brothers and sisters, think of what you were when you were called. Not many of you were wise by human standards; not many were influential; not many were of noble birth" (1 Corinthians 1:26). Our sovereign God has the audacity of preaching the good news to those who are hidden—the unwise, unimportant, and ignoble.

Preparation

Perhaps most obviously, there is the gift of preparation in the seasons when we are concealed. We are being made ready for something as yet not made known to us. Interestingly, David's long years between his anointing and his appointing were over a decade. God prepared David and his mighty men to lead Israel through the desperately arduous war games they endured in those hidden desert years. Saul likely never realized that his hunting David was being used by God to make a king and leader out of David. Every battle, every deprivation, and every strategy prepared David to take the kingdom's mantle. These unseen years became a hidden forge that helped to mold him into a man after God's own heart (Acts 13:22).

But it is the earliest story of David's young life that speaks most to my impatient heart about the deep preparation of being hidden. The prophet Samuel, mourning over God's rejection of King Saul, was directed by God to fill his horn with oil (the mode of anointing) and make haste to Jesse's house, where he would find the new king among Jesse's sons. Here, we pick up the story midstream:

When they arrived, Samuel saw Eliab and thought, "Surely the Lord's anointed stands here before the Lord."

But the Lord said to Samuel, "Do not consider his appearance or his height, for I have rejected him. The Lord does not look at the things people look at. People look at the outward appearance, but the Lord looks at the heart."

Then Jesse called Abinadab and had him pass in front of Samuel. But Samuel said, "The Lord has not chosen this one either." Jesse then had Shammah pass by, but Samuel said, "Nor has the Lord chosen this one." Jesse had seven of his sons pass before Samuel, but Samuel said to him, "The Lord has not chosen these." So he asked Jesse, "Are these all the sons you have?"

"There is still the youngest," Jesse answered. "He is tending the sheep."

Samuel said, "Send for him; we will not sit down until he arrives."

So he sent for him and had him brought in. He was glowing with health and had a fine appearance and handsome features.

Then the Lord said, "Rise and anoint him; this is the one."

So Samuel took the horn of oil and anointed him in the presence of his brothers. (1 Samuel 16:6–13)

Scripture implies that Jesse had brought all his sons to the prophet—after all, a house call from the esteemed prophet Samuel was no garden-variety experience. Jesse proudly paraded out his sons, surely hoping for the destiny-making declaration: "Behold the head that will wear the crown." However, with each passing form of tall embodied glory, the Lord instructed, *Don't look at his outward appearance, Samuel; look at his heart. He is not My chosen one.* In other words, God doesn't see as the world sees. His omniscient X-ray vision penetrates to the deeper stuff, to what is hidden beneath physical beauty, physical prowess, or even irresistible personality. Some of the wisest people I have ever known have been wrapped in it-takes-time-to-penetrate introversion. Some of the most caring and kind souls have been hidden in social awkwardness. Sometimes the most interesting person in the room is sitting in the corner of it. Sometimes it's easy to overlook these gems. But we're not alone in that all-too-human tendency. It gives me great hope that even the prophet Samuel, who walked in close concert with God, *at times* focused on the wrong validating elements. Speaking of which, let's dip back into the waters of his story.

Finally, surely feeling confused, the prophet asked Jesse, "Are these all the sons you have?"

Jesse sheepishly admitted he had one more son—the baby, who was out in the field.

My theatrical brain fills in the blanks of Jesse's subtext: *Surely it's not David. If you think it's David, think again.*

I've always puzzled over why Jesse didn't remember David. Was David seen more as a pseudo-servant than as a son? Did Jesse discount David because of his age or view him as the black sheep? All are possibilities, since the Hebrew word Jesse used, translated as "youngest," is *qatan*, meaning small, young, unimportant, the last.[10] Apparently, David was so out of sight and so out of mind that Jesse thought of him—in this case—as outside the family's inner circle, unworthy of consideration. Unworthy of inclusion. David was so forgotten by his own family that Samuel had to ask his father if he had overlooked anyone for the spiritual parade—"Are these all?"

Rejection and exclusion can create deep spiritual and psychological wounds. In fact, recent studies report that "an experience of rejection and an experience of physical pain can both activate the same areas of the brain. . . . We all have a fundamental need to belong to a group. When we get rejected, this need becomes destabilized and the disconnection we feel adds to our emotional pain."[11]

When we sense rejection from people who should accept us, include us, and see us rightly—especially family or friends—well, the poison is distilled rather than diluted. We don't need to go down the wormholes of rejection and exclusion to understand the septic wound these unholy twins cause, but I would be remiss if I didn't write these words:

> **In Christ, we are not rejected, forgotten, excluded, or marginalized. Even when no one else affirms us, Jesus does.**

In Christ, we are not rejected, forgotten, excluded, or marginalized. In Him, we are accepted in the Beloved. In Him, we have a seat at the table. In Him, we are considered. And even when no one else affirms us, Jesus does.

Fellow sojourner, if you have ever been forgotten, resist the temptation to misinterpret that forgottenness. And be careful about doing faulty math on your season of forgottenness (by others), thinking, *God has forgotten me too. I'm invisible to God.* A season of "human forgottenness" may be forging something in you of great worth spiritually. Your season of hiddenness may be preparing you in ways you can't yet conceive.

It may be preparing you by inoculating you from seeing as the world sees. And, friend, I am not sure we have ever needed a heavenward, "fix your eyes" view more than we need it now. Our world is in desperate need of Christ followers to say prayers instead of post insults, to let go of offenses instead of making a list and checking it twice. To reach across the divide rather than blowing up spiritual bridges. To turn the other cheek rather than to prepare a backhand slap. And sometimes it is our hiddenness, our pain, our forgottenness—used and transformed in His nail-scarred hands—that give us such rare gifts.

When you have been forgotten, you tend not to forget others. When you have been on the periphery, you'll tend to notice those on the periphery. When God chooses to bring you in from the shadows and the field, you tend to focus on Him, not man, as the door opener. This will surely develop an urgency to be one after God's own heart. Don't short-circuit the gift of hidden preparation.

In a much smaller way I had a season of hidden preparation as well. Right out of college, I auditioned for a Broadway revival and learned I was up for one of the leads. Ultimately, I did not land that role but was cast as that role's understudy, meaning I would go on when that actor could not. The whole thing was a master class in preparation: I apprenticed under someone with far more tools in her tool kit. She was an oak; I was an acorn. I was very much hidden in her shadow, but it wasn't bad; it was beneficial. And when I finally stepped out and played the role, which I did close to fifty times, I had been made ready. Though I was a bit whiny when I didn't land the role, being hidden was the Lord's gift to me.

I was being prepared for an assignment that God had prepared for me from the foundation of the world. You are, too, friend. Don't rush the process. Waiting time in Christ is never wasted time. Never.

Let God prepare you, making you ready beforehand.

Protection

Just as important as preparation is protection. Emotionally, spiritually, and even physically, seasons of hiddenness are protective. For example, Moses' parents physically hid him at home, and they were commended for their daring act in Hebrews 11: "By faith Moses' parents hid him for three months after he was born, because they saw he was no ordinary child, and they were not afraid of the king's edict" (v. 23). Without his parents hiding him away, ignoring the king's edict, would Moses have survived to lead God's people?

I could sometimes weep at what exposure and visibility are stealing from us and from those who come after us. One of the fears of this generation is that they might become a meme, a laughingstock, should something be put out on the internet that might make someone's online shame show. I think of the writers, pastors, and thinkers who will be stunted because of some of the ill fruits that come along with overexposure. They will step out—or be forced to step out—before their time, wilting in the premature visibility, and will never step out again. Oftentimes, when God hides us, He is protecting us from overexposure.

Oftentimes, when God hides us, He is protecting us from overexposure.

One of the dear friends of my life is an extremely accomplished photographer. He is credited with several pioneering breakthroughs in the way film was processed from film to paper during the heyday of analog (rather than digital) photography. His images were regularly featured in national campaigns, and before we befriended each other, I rode the subways with his beautiful art, never the wiser but, still, stunned at the images I saw.

One of the things I recall about Brad was the way he developed his work; his art wasn't just about capturing the image but about the way the image was developed. Once, I got a peek inside his dark room; it looked for all the world like a brilliant scientist's lab as images came to life in states of light and dark. If the image was blown out by light in such a way that distorted the image, it had to go. Too much light at the wrong time caused a blurriness that rendered the shot unusable.

I think the same thing can happen to us; too much light at the wrong time, and the image is distorted. Don't chase premature exposure; it may render the beauty-filled image of God's work in your life as less than what it could be if you simply waited for the protection He offers. I cannot help but return to the hidden black whelk, protected and whole because of a long season of hiddenness.

Potency

Next, we move to potency. Some purposes are most potent when completed in obscurity. Call to mind the Old Testament spies, who were sent to scope out Jericho in the promised land. I imagine an ancient *Mission Impossible* movie. The spies were told to take in the lay of the land and then report back to Joshua about the city's status. The spiritual secret agents' job could only be properly fulfilled if done in secret. In fact, this is where we see the astonishing story of Rahab, the prostitute turned protector.

Then Joshua son of Nun secretly sent two spies from Shittim.

The spies headed to Jericho and landed at the home of Rahab, a prostitute. Once the king discovered that the Israelites had come to reconnoiter his city and were hiding at Rahab's, he sent word to hand the spies over posthaste—"but she had taken them up to the roof and hidden them under the stalks of flax she had laid out on the roof" (Joshua 2:6). When officials came looking for the spies at her house, Rahab continued the ruse by lying about where they had gone, essentially sending the officials on a wild-goose chase.

As the pursuers followed a false lead, Rahab told the spies,

> I know that the LORD has given you this land. . . . We have heard how the LORD dried up the water of the Red Sea. . . . Our hearts melted in fear and everyone's courage failed because of you, for the LORD your God is God in heaven above and on the earth below.
>
> Now then, please swear to me by the LORD that you will show kindness to my family, because I have shown kindness to you. Give me a sure sign that you will spare the lives of my father and mother, my brothers and sisters, and all who belong to them—and that you will save us from death. (vv. 9–13)

In their gratitude, the spies agreed, promising to save Rahab and her family when the Israelites moved into the land.

Rahab directed them through a window and lowered them down by rope. "Go to the hills so the pursuers will not find you," she said. "Hide yourselves there three days until they return, and then go on your way" (v. 16).

This cat-and-mouse exploit was absolutely necessary. If the spies had been discovered, their heads would have been on pikes faster than the weather changes at the Outer Banks, and their crucial message to their people would have remained undelivered. The spies had to be hidden to accomplish their assignment.

This divine hiddenness brings to mind missionaries who

cannot even speak the name of the countries to which they are sent. They must remain hidden, because to be exposed by the world might mean the cessation of the work God has called them to.

Perfect Timing

Finally, there are seasons when God hides something on purpose so that it will be revealed at just the correct time. Think of the atoning, sacrificial death of Jesus Christ. Paul wrote, "You see, *at just the right time*, when we were still powerless, Christ died for the ungodly" (Romans 5:6). At just the right time in history, according to all the prophecies that had been spoken but hidden for ages, God revealed His Son at an exact, specific moment in time.

> **There are seasons when God hides something on purpose so that it will be revealed at just the correct time.**

Even Peter said we are released from suffering after a little while; in other words, there is a time limit—the clock runs out—on our most difficult seasons. And when it runs out, our good, good Father does something stupendous: "The God of all grace, who called you to his eternal glory in Christ, after you have suffered a little while, will himself restore you and make you strong, firm and steadfast" (1 Peter 5:10).

During a recent season of suffering, I prayed such simple, childlike things: "I just want it to stop. Help. Please." My soul's lament harmonized with the laments of the Psalms, and I questioned, "How long, oh Lord? How long?" This spiritual wail wasn't for a God-on-command as much as it was my twisting heart's cry for a God-at-hand, one who would bring the emotional tumult to an end. To fast-forward the clock on suffering.

I wish I had easy-to-swallow answers for the questions that surface from our souls during seasons of suffering. There is so much my heart cannot answer because it does not know. What I do know, however, I know like my own name: Jesus is transforming me in the storm. I come out different than I went in. My faith-grasp is strengthened as I hold on to the mast of His strength. My wisdom is sharpened when I learn to wisely weather a storm. My hope is made resilient when I wait—and finally witness—the Source of real hope bursting forth like the rising sun. All of that takes time. After decades of walking with Jesus, I have learned to trust His timing. He sees things I can't. He knows things I don't. He is fighting things I can't conquer. He's leveling old ruins and laying new foundations. He is working things out for His own purposes and to His own ends for His own glory. Therefore, I can rest knowing "my times are in [God's] hand" (Psalm 31:15 NKJV). His timing regarding my "times" is always perfect. He sees and knows all. My job is to stay on His heels and in His shadow.

> **Even when you can't see the answer—or any answer—it doesn't mean it isn't right around the corner.**

A small encouragement from my heart to yours, friend, if you're in a season of waiting: even when you can't see the answer—or any answer—it doesn't mean it isn't right around the corner. Imagine Mary Magdalene standing outside an empty tomb on that first Easter morn, talking to a man she thought was a gardener but was, in fact, the resurrected Jesus. The answer was right there, about to be revealed, though she couldn't "see" it yet. If you feel as if your life is simply a series of corners you can't quite see around, nestle into the fact that you serve a God who sees around corners.

Posthumous Rewards

At the beginning of this chapter, I told you about discovering Mr. Etheridge in a worn photo while touring the Outer Banks aquarium. After that, I got a closer look at his (and the Lifesavers') incredible, intrepid lives at the Pea Island Cookhouse Museum in Manteo, North Carolina. I saw pictures of commendation and artifacts from the Lifesavers' time on the island. And I learned that in 1996, one hundred years after their upending work, the Coast Guard issued a posthumous commendation for the entire battalion.[12]

On a perfect spring day earlier this year, I walked to a traffic circle to see the bronze statue of Richard Etheridge erected there. As cars sped by, I stood in the shadow of a great, hidden piece of history. While some reasons for the Lifesavers' hiddenness from history are obvious, others remain only in God's sovereign purview. I looked up at Etheridge's edifice and thought, *Some things will never make full sense this side of heaven. This is why it is so important to live this life knowing that what we experience here is not the end of the story. We must live with our eyes up and remember that the story goes on.*

Maybe you, too, are serving in obscurity, shaded from the view of others. Here's a question I've been mulling over for a while: What if God never calls us out for our huge *ta-da* moment in the spotlight? What if we allow God to form in us a desire to do the work of the ministry without acclaim, "as unto the Lord" (Colossians 3:23 ASV)? What if we actually pursue hidden faithfulness, leaving outward fruitfulness up to Him? Maybe we will see some of that spiritual fruit on this side of eternity, and maybe we won't. But we know we will be rewarded posthumously, as Richard Etheridge and his faithful crew were, when we see Him face-to-face and He recognizes us as His own, speaking the words we long to hear: "Well done, good and faithful servant."

Well done.

Father, I confess today that I chafe under the ministry of waiting and holy hiddenness. I have an impatient soul. My feet itch to move. I hunger for the hit of the next thing. I am anxious to move on from this season, assuming I'm stuck in a place of "nothingness," forgetting that You are never up to "nothing." Help me to surrender to—and even delight in—this ministry. This season. This call of deepening roots. Of strengthening spiritual arms. Of preparation for the next season. I whisper back to You the waiting words of Scripture.

I wait for You, Lord, and keep Your way.

I will rest in You, Lord, and wait patiently for You.

I wait for You, Lord—my soul does wait, and in Your Word I do hope.

My heart longs to long for what You long for. To will what You will. When my own heart tempts me to run ahead, help me stop and pause into maturity. By faith, I thank You for coverage and concealment. Always, Your child.

CHAPTER 5

The Hidden Tides

The hidden things belong to the LORD our God.
DEUTERONOMY 29:29 CSB

His mother had felt led to pray that day, burdened about her youngest son, who was away at the Carolina coast on a youth group retreat. Like a child who pulls upon a mother's skirt, the call to prayer wouldn't be ignored, so she prayed without ceasing without even knowing the reason. She knew beyond a shadow of a doubt that the urge to intercede concerned her son, who is now my husband. Since this was before the age of social media, some time would pass before she and her husband heard the news: their son had been caught in a dangerous riptide, and, though he was fine, it had taken two lifeguards (with a third on the way) to pull him out of the Atlantic rip currents and deliver him safely to shore.

We've been looking out for rips for twenty-five years.

On the Outer Banks, the signs are everywhere warning of hidden danger: the dreaded rip current. Rip currents are strong currents that run perpendicular to the beach and can suck even a strong swimmer a thousand feet out to sea in a mere minute. In fact, 80 percent of all water rescues in the Banks are due to rip currents. Here, they happen most often when a sandbar splits open, causing a huge channel of water to run out to sea. When the flags on the beach fly red, which they often do, no one—no matter how skilled—is allowed to be in the water. The red flags are a warning that there are unseen dangers underneath the surface.[1]

So far we've talked about the glory of the hidden-with-Christ life, the power in choosing a hidden life unhurried and unimpeded by the drive to be known by the world. We've even talked about the unique gifts the Lord deepens in us during seasons of hidden, quiet waiting.

Now we're going to shift our perspective a bit. We're going to turn the shell and attempt to peer within, looking for things beneath the waterlines of our lives, things we think we've hidden from the Lord (impossible!): false forces, damaging beliefs—rip currents, if you will—that, left unchecked, have the power to move our life's ship way off course.

Scripture says, "There is nothing hidden that will not be disclosed" (Luke 8:17). In context, this verse is talking about two distinct things: the hidden kingdom being revealed (blessed revelation!) and the seriousness of the final judgment (serious business!). Though this verse is both an invitation and a warning, I've learned there is an incredible opportunity for transformation nestled in its words; disclosure can bring a beautiful healing closure. I want to surrender to Jesus' work in unseen places. Most of us want to know if there is an unholy undertow that threatens to undo us. So let's ask Jesus to encounter us in the oceanic trenches of our lives—those deep places that are difficult to plumb—because it is there that we need Him the most, and it is there that He graciously meets us and sees us.

Our Concealed Character for this chapter is perhaps a bit of a left turn. We're looking at an unnamed women mentioned in the Passion Week account of Jesus. As far as we know, she never surrendered to Jesus, but certainly encountered Him in a hidden place in her life—her dreams. Here I imagine her perspective in the days between Jesus' death and resurrection.

CONCEALED CHARACTERS

Pilate's Wife

I see I am not the only one the Nazarene troubled. I am not much used to being troubled.

I had heard of Him before I dreamed of Him. My women whispered rumors of the strange teacher who was often seen teaching day after day, rarely, if ever, alone. He did not stand distant from the poor, the young, or even women. Strange.

To be the center of such a clamor of people and never once to use the gift of being loved to further oneself is . . . strange.

He was taller in my dream. Almost near to a giant. A giant

who held my husband's palace—the prefect's palace—in one hand like it was a child's toy. And, in my dream, Pontius, my husband, stepped out and pierced the hand that held our toy palace. And the Nazarene's blood flowed until it became a sea, until it rose the earth over and broke our house apart like it was made of feathers. My dream meant that the Nazarene would destroy our kingdom; that is why I sent word to my husband while he judged the Nazarene. "Have nothing to do with this man, for I have been much troubled in a dream on account of Him"—that was only the half of it. I have never been so troubled. I am troubled still.

My husband tried and tried and tried again to let Him loose, finding no fault in Him. But the people, in the end, must be heeded. My husband told me that the Nazarene never raged. Never begged. Even seemed to pity him. Imagine pitying the man who holds your life in his hands.

I see now that it was the other way around.

And even with Him gone the way of all who rise against rule, I see Him in my dreams. Though dead, the Nazarene troubles me as if still alive.

Maybe the whispered rumors spoken of Him are true.[2]

Even with what I hope is a bit of sanctified imagining regarding Pilate's wife's dream, I think the heart of it beats true. Here we see a woman accustomed to privilege and power, a woman who, no doubt, did *not* worship the one true God, yet something in the most hidden place—her dreams—so disturbed her, so moved her, so upset her, that she sent word to her husband, the prefect of the occupied territory, to have nothing to do with the source of that disturbance: Jesus. Pilate's wife must've known something about Him was deeply different and realized He presented a danger to her husband's standing.

I have always wondered if her dream and her warning about that dream might be part of the reason Pilate tried with everything in him to let Jesus go. This is a question I must save for eternity, but it is clear: something about this Jesus so upset the order of things that even a woman with no belief found herself troubled beneath the surface.

Struggling with Spiritual Riptides

Paul, the power apostle who possessed an unimpeachable intellect and unswerving commitment to Christ Jesus in every manner in life, still wrote these honest words in Romans 7:19–20: "For I do not do the good I want to do, but the evil I do not want to do—this I keep on doing. Now if I do what I do not want to do, it is no longer I who do it, but it is sin living in me that does it." Later Paul exclaimed, "Who will rescue me from this body that is subject to death?" (v. 24). Romans 7 is a master class in law and grace, but in these verses we have the apostle speaking of the "struggle of human effort under the law" and expressing the battle between good and evil.[3]

Like Paul, we innately understand this battle. Who among us doesn't know the wringing twist, the sprung trap of sinful, destructive choices? We know (and sometimes don't know) there can be spiritual riptides—attitudes, brokenness, and sin patterns that, without a lifeguard, will take us under. Jesus knows how to interrupt the undertow and rescue us from those rough-and-tumble breakers.

The reasons we get snagged in a spiritual undertow are complex. Often, the reasons cannot be easily reduced; they are not a singular tonic note nor an easily diagrammable thesis statement. Reasons for anything are like ancient tells, layer upon layer upon layer, each era's reasons thrown upon the heap, until the root is buried as deep as the earthen core. Such was the case with my reasons.

At one point during the recent season of difficulty, I noticed an uptick in my tendency to spend copious amounts of time on social media. The whole thing crept up on me, like a riptide might. I'm not proud of it; I'm just being real about it. As a person who has long been consumed by creating and crafting in analog, and as someone not really given to excess, this was a new type of captivity. Numbing instead of noticing. This consuming and observing and commenting upon became a counterfeit lifeline, tethering me to modes of avoidance rather than the Messiah's deliverance. Rather than facing the hard work of healing—of sitting with the damage that lay underneath the piers of my life—I scrolled and scrolled for hours on end, hoping to be consoled, hoping to short-circuit the process of healing, and hoping the Lord would not require a deep dive. Of course, He did—He always goes to the seabed. Always.

I've spent some time wondering why it's so easy to run to something so antilife. So counterfeit.

We all know by now that social media is primed to keep us scrolling, and those sticky algorithms are actually changing our brains. A landmark report recently detailed some of the deleterious effects of social media on developing brains.[4] We become addicted to the dopamine hits of novelty, hence we keep looking and scrolling, even when the content is negative, even when our wiser mind screams, *Turn it off! Put it down!* Just one more TikTok dance. Just one more Instagram heart. Just one more feeling of indignant offense. Just one more text-to-be-answered-now. I truly believe decades from now, we will weep at the great experiment we unleashed upon ourselves and our children.[5] I am grateful for folks in this particular space who are encouraging fasting from social media for periods of time or joining mindful social media movements.

I've been leaning into the whispers of the Lord in my own life, as it regards social media's riptide influence. I've heard the Lord whisper internally, *Refrain. For this moment, refrain.*

But, Lord, how will they know about that übercool moment with übercool people if I don't post?

Refrain.

I've got to say something. My opinion should be heard.

Refrain.

How can I humble-brag about that positive review/interaction/ commendation?

Refrain.

Set the record straight.

Refrain.

Shouldn't I be aware of what is going on, though?

Refrain.

If I don't post most days, algorithmic visibility will drop, and I'll lose opportunity.

Refrain.

Now, friends, I don't feel led to refrain all the time as it relates to social media—hardly. But I have felt the Lord asking me to walk in this discipline more and more. When He asks me to refrain, I sense that He is helping me to exercise agency over a complex force that so easily entangles itself like seaweed around my feet and drowns me.

And perhaps there is a holy refrain—a repeating melody of truth—that I hear in my heart more clearly when I refrain, when I am willing to live counterculturally.

In contrast to a world that values and celebrates social media influencers, God often calls the *non*influencers—which, in our day and age, has an uncomfortable resonance. One of the most interesting prophecies of Jesus is found in Isaiah 42:2, which says, "He will not shout or cry out, or raise his voice in the streets." In other words, when the Messiah came, He would be quite unlike other kings of the earth, ruling like a bellicose and demanding human might, requiring loud human crowing and worldly crowns.[6] Rather, He would eschew the clamor of the crowd for intimacy with His Father and followers.

We see in the Gospels that during His earthly ministry, Jesus ran from making a name for Himself, as we understand it, and spent His time teaching His disciples to hallow the name of our Father in heaven. Even though Jesus has "the name that is above every name" (Philippians 2:9), He often chose a hidden life of humility and service.

In a world that tempts me to make a name for myself, this countercultural approach to life and ministry, as exhibited by the Son of God, is a heart-checker. *Where might I refrain? Where might I flee from the idea that visibility is synonymous with favor?*

Savior > Social Media

Recently, I did some digging on the phenomenon of doomscrolling: the captivity that happens when we can't stop looking at media cycles, even though we feel a sense of impending dread. Why are we primed for negative capture, particularly in this way?

Some researchers suggest that "because negativity is often associated with fear or danger, and positivity with security and safety, at a cognitive level, a person automatically pays more attention to unpleasant (negative) than to pleasant (positive) information. This psychological phenomenon is called the Negativity bias."[7]

I fooled myself into thinking I would see something on socials—especially as my feed is almost exclusively Christocentric—that might spark healing or insight or a rescue from the season of struggle I was in. But the medicine I was using was sickening me rather than healing me. It exacerbated my wounds; it didn't heal them—in part because my feed consisted of empty calories. Food of dubious quality. It's hard to fix your mind on social media and the Savior in equal parts.

There's such a wily trap in believing that reading about spiritual things is the same as participating in spiritual things. "Liking" something that seems like the kingdom is not the same as developing a heart that beats for the kingdom. In some ways all this social media overload was a deflection technique, as I was trying to stave off the call to go beneath the surface with Jesus. I could hear the words of Paul echoing in my spiritual ears: "Who will rescue me from this body that is subject to death?" Who indeed?

Like the ballad Jesus sang on the sandy beach the day I discovered the hidden whelk, I can almost hear the magisterial melody again. I can almost hear him singing over us, *I know you are hurting right now, My child, but some of the things you think will help are actually hurting you. And there are some things I want to go with you to the ocean floor on. I want you to create space. Margin.*

You are not your social media curations. You are not what you build for consumption. And you are not what you consume.

The more miles I get on my spiritual tires, the more I pray the prayer of Paul in Ephesians: "I pray that the eyes of your heart may be enlightened in order that you may know the hope to which he has called you" (1:18). *Lord, do for us what we cannot do for ourselves. Help us hold the view, help us see and understand and meditate on the glory hiding in plain sight, even when our worlds have been stripped down to the studs. Especially then.*

Friend, you are seen by the God who sees you.

Lift up your eyes and hold on. The One who can help us is coming to the rescue. Friend, you are seen by the God who sees you.

Hidden on Purpose for His Purposes

After walking with Jesus for thirty-five years, I more quickly allow Him to load my bones on His shoulders and carry me wherever He will. I'm trusting that if the Lord calls me to a quiet, hidden place in Him, then it is for my ultimate good and for His glory. To "kick against the goads" (Acts 9:5 NKJV) is to bruise more than my body but my heart and mind as well. Surrender has become a friend to me; trust, a dear family member; and obedience, a brother-in-arms.

This has not always been so. I have chafed against God's timing far too many times and reaped for myself the ill fruits of such a fight. Sometimes this happened because I went against my internal seafaring compass and turned my ship by degrees heading for the dangerous shoals, not knowing I was heading for a crash. It was then that I reoriented my heart to the sky's North Star and trusted again in His sovereign deliberateness.

As I have lived seasons of exposure and seasons of hiddenness, I find myself leaning on and longing more than ever before for His ways, His timing, and His will, whether I'm seen by thousands or none at all. I know that I am seen by Him, and that makes all the difference.

Escaping a Riptide

Today, I'm back at the Outer Banks, looking at the red flags flying, snapping like warnings in the wind. No swimmers, no matter how strong, will be allowed to wade in the water. If you challenge the sea to a duel in weather like this, you will lose. It causes me to think back on the flip side of my husband's riptide kerfuffle, as I watch the waters froth, foam, and beat the shore with the fury of the ages.

While his mother was praying for him back in 1986, Jonathan remembers another side of the story. While he was bodysurfing, he and his friend caught the same wave. Jonathan's friend caught the crest while he was sucked out to sea in the opposite direction. He remembers screaming, "Help!" as he wasn't a robust swimmer. I can only imagine the terror as he realized that the water was well over his head—there was no touching bottom anymore—and he was still being sucked out to sea. Drowning was the probable outcome.

At age thirteen, he didn't know to swim parallel to the shore, perpendicular to the riptide. He didn't know how to conserve his energy and tread water, refusing to directly fight the rip current itself. It took two lifeguards, with a third (and a rescue winch) on the way to get him back to safety. He was exhausted from trying to stay afloat, finally surrendering to the lifeguards' strength, and they got him back to the safety of shore. I don't know their names, but I wish I could thank them for putting their own lives at risk to save my one-day husband's.

As I look back on the season I was caught in the social media rip current, I think of the natural wisdom of escaping one in real life. What catches me the most is the instruction to wait out the worst churn and then swim *across* the current, not directly against it. From my earliest visits to the Outer Banks, I was reminded: swim across, not against. You swim toward a different goal, a place counterintuitive to your instinct. You turn around, in a manner of speaking, which is a fabulous way of describing repentance. As I began to reenter a place where I could let the spiritual healing begin, I knew not to fight against social media's death grip on me but to refrain, and to turn my eyes and swim toward somewhere else, to Someone else. And as I did, I noticed that the Ultimate Lifeguard already had me spotted; He was already on the way.

Help was already on the way.

Jesus, we cannot begin to comprehend the rip currents of our lives without seeing through Your eyes. We can't see things that tangle our legs from underneath and sweep us out to sea, sometimes before we can even scream "Help!" Often we can't identify the pain, the problem, the proclivity. The undertow.

So come help us, Lord. We welcome a holy confrontation. We need You to be the Ultimate Lifeguard who meets us in our place of trouble and brings us safely back to shore.

Jesus, we fall upon Your mercy and all-knowing wisdom. We envision You walking on the water to a sinking Peter, reaching out Your hand in rescue. Reach and rescue our sinking hearts, now, Lord, before we drown in the unseen undertow. We need You beyond all needing, and we put all our trust in Your power. Amen and amen.

CHAPTER 6

What Lies Beneath

"There is nothing concealed that
will not be disclosed."
MATTHEW 10:26

My mind couldn't take it in. *This cannot be happening*, I thought. I tried restarting my computer (hitting the power button far more violently than needed) to see if the file would magically reappear. When that didn't work, I berated my brain, bit my lip, and conducted a manic search of my computer's contents—"Outer Banks," "Lost Colony," "Ocracoke," "Hatteras Island," "Pea Island Lifesavers," "Colossae"—all to no avail. In an already jammed month, in the middle of a move, I had lost a whole chapter and a pertinent chunk of the necessary work for the book I now write. Stories, scriptures, scaffolding—all vanished into the vortex of computerdom.

I wanted to weep at what had been lost. *What a waste*, I thought, desperately scribbling the fast-fading details from memory. It felt like a violent storm spout descending with no warning, leaving nothing in its wake: wisps of thoughts, echoes of words, phantoms of stories. The anxiety was palpable. How would I ever recover the hidden work that makes writing possible?

Frustrated at the empty search results, I surrendered and painfully started to click-clack on the computer keys (making sure AutoSave was on this time). I began to do the hidden work—again. And again.

I often wonder if Baruch ever felt the same.

The One Who Swung the Stylus

Along with Isaiah, Jeremiah is a preferred prophet of the Old Testament. A priest who prophesied to a remnant of the Southern Kingdom for forty (or more) years, Jeremiah is easy to empathize with. The youthful, weeping, and emotional prophet is tender and touchable.

And while the book of Jeremiah has many beautiful points of connection, this prophetic book also feels a bit like a biblical version of the movie *Titanic*, with Jeremiah prophesying that a direct collision with the glacier of captivity is quickly approaching, while most everyone else is noshing on baked Alaska.

And by his side, a bit like a spiritual second lieutenant, was Baruch, Jeremiah's scribe.

Scribes were an interesting bunch in biblical history. This

literary cohort was skilled in recording important happenings as well as interpreting the law and moving in and out of geopolitical arenas. They taught the Torah and other Jewish literature, served as political advisers or diplomats, and functioned as wise sages, elders, and judges.[1] Think of these writers as poet laureates meet power attorneys. They have an illustrious role to play all the way through the pages of Scripture, and Baruch was numbered among their throng.

In the fourth year of the reign of King Jehoiakim of Judah, while the prophet Jeremiah was weeping and warning, God commanded Baruch to record all the prophecies regarding His people.

> "Take a scroll and write on it all the words that I have spoken to you against Israel and Judah and all the nations, from the day I spoke to you, from the days of Josiah until today. It may be that the house of Judah will hear all the disaster that I intend to do to them, so that every one may turn from his evil way, and that I may forgive their iniquity and their sin."
>
> Then Jeremiah called Baruch the son of Neriah, and Baruch wrote on a scroll at the dictation of Jeremiah all the words of the LORD that he had spoken to him. (Jeremiah 36:2–4 ESV)

Surely Baruch swallowed hard when Jeremiah delivered the news, hands shaking to handle such holy words. Can't you just imagine Baruch, working from sunup to sundown, his hand cramping around the scribe's stylus, his fingertips stained with the precious ink? How deliberately Jeremiah must have spoken God's declarations so that Baruch didn't miss a word from day one.

Though we are not exactly sure when God gave the directive, we know it encompassed the beginning of Jeremiah's ministry to the current day. It was delicate dictation that I imagine took eons. This compendium of God's confrontation to His people would have been more akin to Tolstoy's *War and Peace* than a summer beach read, since, by the time the directive was demanded, Jeremiah had been prophesying for years. I can almost imagine Baruch's final, relieved exhale when the last letter of the last word was inscribed, and he dusted it with sand and rolled up the scroll, delicately handing the precious work to Jeremiah. Baruch surely deserved an extreme Sabbath rest after such a gargantuan task.

But the story of Baruch's hidden handiwork doesn't end there. Mondays are inevitable, and when Baruch reported back to work, the prophet added another task to Baruch's holy to-do list.

Jeremiah ordered Baruch, saying, "I am banned from going to the house of the LORD, so you are to go, and on a day of fasting in the hearing of all the people in the LORD's house you shall read the words of the LORD from the scroll that you have written at my dictation. You shall read them also in the hearing of all the men of Judah who come out of their cities. It may be that their plea for mercy will come before the LORD, and that every one will turn from his evil way, for great is the anger and wrath that the LORD has pronounced against this people." And Baruch the son of Neriah did all that Jeremiah the prophet ordered him about reading from the scroll the words of the LORD in the LORD's house. (vv. 5–8 ESV)

Oh, my heavenly stars. It's easy to speed by these sentences like a bullet train, isn't it? But let's pull the emergency brake for a moment. First, Baruch was being asked to step outside his normal capacity. Though we know scribes sometimes stepped into these spheres, it is apparent that, in this case, Jeremiah's job was prophesying, and Baruch's was writing.

Baruch knew that Jeremiah's voice was about as welcomed as screaming goats at the temple; people, powerful or plain, don't especially like being told that their spiritual ships are going to hit the glacier and there is almost certainly nothing they can do to stop the crash. No wonder Jeremiah was often threatened and once even thrown into a cistern (Jeremiah 38:6). Jeremiah reiterated his outcast state by telling Baruch that he had been banned from the house of the Lord, so he instructed Baruch, in essence, "You do it. The hot potato is yours." Talk about a way to kick off the workweek! Though I bet his knees were knocking louder than coconut shells in a hurricane, Baruch obeyed.

Here comes the second sticky wicket: Baruch was to declare this judgmental, magisterial monologue in front of all the men of Judah, using not just his hands but his voice.

And that's when things started to go from sinking soil to quicksand. Some of the governmental muckety-mucks caught wind of the scroll's reading at the Lord's house, and they asked Baruch to read the scroll again in their hearing. Baruch obliged; it's a wonder he didn't develop laryngitis the way he was declaiming and declaring all over the place, in Jeremiah's place. At the end of the second reading, Baruch didn't receive a standing ovation but looks of abject terror:

> When they heard all the words, they turned one to another in fear. And they said to Baruch, "We must report all these words to the king." Then they asked Baruch, "Tell us, please, how did you write all these words? Was it at his dictation?" Baruch

answered them, "He dictated all these words to me, while I wrote them with ink on the scroll." Then the officials said to Baruch, "Go and hide, you and Jeremiah, and let no one know where you are." (36:16–19 ESV)

Scripture doesn't tell us where Jeremiah and Baruch hid, but I can imagine their conversations, can't you? "Way to throw me under the bus, Jeremiah. Speaking isn't exactly in my wheelhouse." I don't know whether they hid in a house, hovel, or cave, but I bet they sweated bullets while they waited for someone to tell them what in God's wide world was going on with that scroll. Eventually they would find out.

Scripture records that the scroll was indeed read in the presence of the king, and at specific intervals—every three or four columns to be exact—the king cut the scroll and threw God's Word into the firepot (v. 23). This interesting detail would make a wonderfully delicious movie scene, because the king didn't just take the scroll and throw the whole part and parcel into the flames—no, Jehoiakim listened to God's words and then deliberately, calculatingly, threw them into the fire. I imagine a *Godfather* mafia don sitting by a campfire burning the evidence of his crimes.

Though those in attendance urged the king not to treat God's guidance with such contempt, Scripture records, "he would not listen to them" (v. 25). And then the king gave the command for someone to find and seize "Baruch the scribe and Jeremiah the prophet. [Notice who gets mentioned first!] But the LORD had hidden them" (v. 26).

Here I wonder about the concealed contents of Baruch's thoughts upon hearing the news.

CONCEALED CHARACTERS

Baruch, the Scribe of Jeremiah the Prophet

Our king is mad—mad as a murder of crows frenzied at fresh meat. Mad as Nebuchadnezzar of Babylon, who will come as sure as the dawn. This is an animal's doings: to burn the words of God as if they were nothing. Turning gold to ash. Bit by bit. They say he sneered and gnashed as he did, slicing the scroll with a dirty dagger, like a fieldhand eviscerating a kill.

God's words. Jeremiah's mouth. My hands. All gone in the fire.

There can be no turning for such a heart. How does the God of all glory hold the remedy for our wound in His hand, yet the king slaps it away? And now the mad king asks for me. He will take my head before it turns snowy. Jeremiah says we will be protected by God's hand. Secured behind His back. Hidden in His pavilion. He tells me to bring my scribal tools, for we will be busy in our hiding place. "We will start again, Baruch. Fire and knives cannot destroy the words of God."

I taste the bile rising like an unwanted tide: I am not made for this. I am a scribe, not a fugitive running from a furious king. I think it, but I dare not say it, as I tell my wife to take the children, to go to her mother's people in the hill country and wait for me there.

Seen, Secure, Free

Imagine if the king of your known world had put a hit out on you, activating every mercenary in the land to look for your inky hands and your specific face. This was the desperation of Baruch's plight. It was so severe that no human hand could shield Baruch and Jeremiah.

I wonder if Baruch and Jeremiah recited the lyrics of Psalm 27 under their breath while the Lord covered them from their adversary, King Jehoiakim:

> For he will hide me in his shelter
> in the day of trouble;
> he will conceal me under the cover of his tent;
> he will lift me high upon a rock.
> And now my head shall be lifted up
> above my enemies all around me,
> and I will offer in his tent
> sacrifices with shouts of joy;
> I will sing and make melody to the LORD.
> Hear, O LORD, when I cry aloud;
> be gracious to me and answer me! . . .
> Teach me your way, O LORD,
> and lead me on a level path
> because of my enemies.
> Give me not up to the will of my adversaries;
> for false witnesses have risen against me,
> and they breathe out violence.
> I believe that I shall look upon the goodness of the LORD
> in the land of the living!
> Wait for the LORD;
> be strong, and let your heart take courage;
> wait for the LORD! (vv. 5–7, 11–14 ESV)

After Baruch and Jeremiah were hidden by God Himself (wherever it may have occurred), there came the word that another exact scroll must be inscribed, after Jeremiah had declared judgment against the king for burning the original scroll:

> Then Jeremiah took another scroll and gave it to Baruch the scribe, the son of Neriah, who wrote on it at the dictation of Jeremiah all the words of the scroll that Jehoiakim king of Judah had burned in the fire. And many similar words were added to them. (36:32 ESV)

This is no phoenix-rising-from-the-ashes, underdog-wins moment. I imagine Baruch looked at the parchment, calculated the cost of recording God's Word under a wrathful king and bit his cheek at the work's dangers. Maybe he even angrily rubbed his hands, conscious of the stiff joints that would once again be put to such a costly, sorrowful endeavor. No one wants to run a marathon only to discover that because of a crooked and vindictive referee, it must be run all over again, with an extra mile added for good measure. Perhaps Baruch swallowed a sob.

Maybe Baruch had to push down the pangs of a panic attack like I did when I lost parts of this book (infinitesimal compared to Scripture). My flesh twisted and turned, angry and childish. Afraid and anxiety ridden. I didn't want to start again.

The *Agains* of God

I don't always take to the word *again*. But sometimes I see something redemptive in it, especially if I can look at the word through a different set of lenses:

> **In God's hands, our *agains* can become our gains.**

Again, ick.

A-gain, interesting.

Maybe in God's hands, our *agains* can become our gains.

When I was in dance class (the least of my three skills, no doubt), the best teachers did a lot of "a-gaining." They knew repetition was the key to developing dance skill. Small mistakes became small corrections. Small corrections became stronger execution. And eventually, a skill to practice became a practiced skill.

Our *agains* can become our gains.

I'm not saying that Baruch needed to write God's words a second time to improve, but I am saying that God had a purpose in Baruch's again, just as He does in ours. There is purpose in the hidden, unseen disciplines we participate in. The things that are unheralded, unwieldy, arduous, difficult, workaday, and costly will be used for God's purpose, especially when we are yielded to the One who knows oh so much better than we do.

I never did find the lost words of the book I now sit writing. I moped a bit, ruminated a bit, bit my lip a bit, and then got back at it. I knew the sovereignty of God would bring purpose from the loss, even purposes I could not yet see. I had only to trust the hard gift of the hidden "again."

The Hard Gift of Hiddenness

In what seems like an odd appendage to Baruch's story, God called Baruch to task for grumbling about the cost of the call on his life.

In fact, He instructed Jeremiah to speak Baruch's words back to Baruch:

> The word that Jeremiah the prophet spoke to Baruch the son of Neriah, when he wrote these words in a book at the dictation of Jeremiah, in the fourth year of Jehoiakim the son of Josiah, king of Judah: "Thus says the LORD, the God of Israel, to you, O Baruch: You said, 'Woe is me! For the LORD has added sorrow to my pain. I am weary with my groaning, and I find no rest.' Thus shall you say to him, Thus says the LORD: Behold, what I have built I am breaking down, and what I have planted I am plucking up—that is, the whole land. And do you seek great things for yourself? Seek them not, for behold, I am bringing disaster upon all flesh, declares the LORD. But I will give you your life as a prize of war in all places to which you may go."
> (Jeremiah 45:1–5 ESV)

In spite of the important and unusual supporting role Baruch played in Judah's national saga, it is this last chapter in our Concealed Character's story that most arrests my heart. The hard gift of a hidden life is staring me right in the face. A hidden life will act as refiner on the invisible matter of the heart, bringing the dross to the surface.

It was God's question of Baruch that handily excavated the dross: "Do you seek great things for yourself? Seek them not."

Yikes. And yes. And amen.

Underneath this faithful, diligent servant's heart lay a driving force, unseen and unknown (apparently even to Baruch himself), and that was the deadly, corrosive effect of pride—evidenced by the fact that Baruch was seeking great things for *himself.* I think it's important to note that we catch no sight of this invasive weed in Jeremiah's narrative; we see only Baruch the scribe doing everything asked of him—not once but twice. Yet God saw the unseen motivations of his heart. He saw what lay beneath, and beneath the appearance of Baruch's faithfulness was the pooling poison of pride.

Pride secretly wars with the Lord when He chooses to use someone in a way in which we would love to be used. Pride is refusing to consider others better than oneself. Pride hunts for the seat of honor while pretending not to care. Pride is appearing to walk obediently in the call of God, like Baruch, while secretly doing it for the kudos. As we witness in Baruch's story, pride hides like a deep-sea leviathan. Outward circumstances don't always tell the full tale; a person with ten million followers might be the humblest person in the room, and one with fifty might be shot through with pride.

Yet, even after God challenged Baruch, He concluded the conversation by telling Baruch that, though He would execute judgment on His people, He would spare Baruch's life. God said to Baruch, "Wherever you go I will let you escape with your life" (v. 5). God showed His care for Baruch's heart by engaging him with a life-altering spoken encounter. But He didn't stop there. God also cared about the very life of the scribe and was intent on doing business with the contents of his heart. As 1 Corinthians 4:5 tells us, the Lord "will bring to light what is hidden in darkness and will expose the motives of the heart."

Truth be told, I don't adore the words the Lord spoke to Baruch after the scribe did the work once, then he did the work again— and then he hid for his life and was carted off into Egypt, with only his very life to show for it. I'd hoped God would have given him a locker-room rouser, not a lashing rebuke. Where are the gold stars, Lord, or at least the promise that, next time, Baruch will get his turn in the spotlight? Maybe as a prophet to the nation himself or maybe as an honored adviser to the king? Instead, our holy, all-knowing God shined His spotlight on the matter of Baruch's heart—and mine—with these revealing words:

Do you seek great things for yourself, Baruch?

Seek. Them. Not.

Do you seek great things for yourself, Allison?

Seek. Them. Not.

Do you seek great things for yourself, friend?

Seek. Them. Not.

Seek out the God of great things first, not the great things of God.

During the writing of this book, these words have become like the waves at my beloved Outer Banks: they keep on coming, forming a rhythmic invitation, again and again and again, washing the sand and dirt off my proverbial heart. This is certainly a part of the refrain Jesus had been singing on that day of the black whelk's discovery. And I think I know why: Baruch's prideful heart beats in my chest too. And it is a heart that needs a good old-fashioned humbling.

My heart is often deceitful and self-focused above all imagining; it wants what it wants. Though none of us love admitting this, secretly we sometimes hope that our hidden faithfulness will lead to public visibility. (Which I have a weird relationship

> **Seek out the God of great things first, not the great things of God.**

with, I might add.) We are often tempted to imagine the quiet work to be God's spiritual ladder for bigger and better spiritual things. As if faithful, hidden communion with the Lord isn't reward enough. As if being a part of the glorious story God is telling isn't honor enough. As if God Himself—His very Self, His gracious involvement of us in His work—isn't enough. As if God isn't *more* than enough. Too often we are like the believers in Colossae who were tempted to add something more than Jesus when, again, what they really needed was more *of* Jesus.

It is clear that somewhere in Baruch's story, he was feeling the need for great things, hoping that his inconvenient, sacrificial, and costly work would earn him bigger and, perhaps, more status-inducing endeavors. He was forgetting that God, and God alone, is reward enough. And God, frankly, called him out on this dangerous internal bentness.

Surely God will elevate me to _____ after the hidden work of _____.

I've got my blanks; Baruch had his; maybe you've got yours too. But when those blanks are filled in with the language of the world, even if they are wrapped up in spiritual-sounding sound bites, they will produce a life that looks like allegiance to ambition rather than allegiance to the Almighty.

When I wrongly believe that followers equal God's favor or platform is evidence of His providential grace, I have replaced the economy of the kingdom with the economy of the world. I am, in effect, seeking great things for myself, wrapped in spiritual language. (Now, His favor *can* include followers and His providential grace *can* be equated with platform—there can be no doubt of this.

But truth be told, the scales have long been out of balance for me and, dare I say, most of us.) The Lord whispered something very precious to my heart in the writing of this book that helped me begin to balance the scales again, and maybe it will help you too:

Daughter, the problem is not in stewarding great things but in seeking them.

When the Lord is doing something in and through us, there is no question that we are to steward what He has entrusted to us in the ways He calls us to (think of the parable of the talents in Matthew 25:14–30). But only the Lord truly knows when our honest stewardship tips over into sneaky status-chasing.

Oh, what a spiritual hurricane the desire for great things can often be! However, there is a blessed eye in the storm. Again, when I reorient myself in the fact that I am hidden with Christ in God, secured and purified by an eternal perspective, safely seen by God and others, I am less reluctant to see the dangers lurking underneath. Sometimes I simply need a good old-fashioned eyewash—anybody remember those? When I was growing up, my mom had a little hard blue vessel that she would fill with fresh water, and she would force me to open my eyes in the clear water. I hated the process but loved the results. Whatever was blocking my view was no challenge to the fresh water rushing into my clouded eye. Want the bad flushed out? Just keep pouring in the good. And, then, clear-eyed, I can ask without fear:

Am I seeking great things for myself?

And because there will be days when the answer, against my best efforts, is yes, I can surrender to answering God's question honestly, sit with the gift of self-awareness His Spirit gives, apply His Word to the hidden motives of my heart, and reembrace the gift of hidden faithfulness. Like Baruch, I can never play hide-and-seek with the Lord. Hebrews 4:13 reminds me, "Nothing in all creation is hidden from God's sight. Everything is uncovered and laid bare before the eyes of him to whom we must give account."

God lays bare the contents of my heart, dividing the soul from the spirit (v. 12). He breaks like a rogue wave, coming up from the sea without warning, landing on the shore of my life, like the Living Word He is. He climbs on the shore, and I have no option but to surrender to His words, sharp as a dagger, bracing as any nor'easter, separating things so intertwined that I can tell neither beginning nor end. He points out the pride of life, the lust of the eyes, and the deep bent toward self. And He invites me to reorient the compass of my life.

He uses my agains. He sees my Baruch heart. He lays me bare.

And, in my life, that is as good and right as a thing has ever been.

Jesus, I know You see it, beating in my chest—this Baruch heart of mine. You know the forces that course through its spiritual chambers, some of which I cannot even identify. They are a part of me, Lord. Some, like Baruch's, are sourced in pride, wrapped in a myriad of culturally acceptable disguises.

Here, I need to re-receive the truth of who You are, and who I am in You. To refuse the definition of myself by myself or anyone else, other than You. Come heal and reveal the forces and patterns in me that are rooted in pain. Damage that I don't have the ability to parse. Ways of self-coping that I learned when I was young. Protective measures for a brutalized heart that I have yet to invite You into.

I invite You into them now. Come gently expose and illuminate. Come shape me the way You want to and make me whole. Amen.

Secure

PART 2

CHAPTER 7

Rooted and Secured

*"I will heal my people and will let them
enjoy abundant peace and security."*

JEREMIAH 33:6

The barrier islands, despite all the efforts to firm them up, are always morphing. I am in shock that Ocracoke (of the Scotch bonnet shell discovery mentioned in chapter 2), a tiny island, still remains and thrives after weathering many a hurricane. Sometimes unusual entities have obstinately deep roots, as do the Outer Banks's revered live oaks.[1]

One of these lovely and bizarre trees, with its low and gnarled branches, has been living for over four hundred years in Manteo's Elizabethan Gardens.[2] Indigenous Americans might have rested in its shade, and some members of the Lost Colony might have done the same, looking for escape from the brutal conditions of Carolina summers. As its venerable state suggests, this live oak possesses the hidden structure to withstand the storm. Its roots dive deep, driven to seek water during dry and trying seasons.

Our first house in Kill Devil Hills is one of the beachfront homes that remain on that particular stretch of the beach, like the last straggly tooth in an old pirate's grin. Many of the other stilted cottages have been culled by hurricanes, but this solitary survivor—rickety though it may be—is surrounded by empty lots. Few want to (or would be allowed to) sink foundations into such shifting sands. Building on any shoreline now is a flip-a-coin proposition: chances are you might weather the storm; chances are you might wilt in it.

Heads or Tails

For most of my life I've lived with an acute sense of the odds. I call it "flip-a-coin living." To the marrow, I know what it is to wonder whether someone is laughing at you or with you. To walk away from a party wondering whether you were winsome or wearying. Whether you were in a place because you were wanted or were simply enough to fit the bill. Whether you were celebrated or merely tolerated. Ah, insecurity. Maybe you've ridden this wild storm's edge as well.

This marrow-deep insecurity doesn't follow me into the performance sphere, strangely. I don't plumb the depths of despair when I don't get the role or the job (although I did when I was younger). I've never been insecure in my marriage relationship. Someone asked me if I had ever been jealous in my marriage. No, not only because my husband has never given me reason to be jealous but also because I'm simply not given to it. There are many delightful spheres where insecurity doesn't track me like a truffle-hunting pig.

But in the social soft spot, my radar often runs red. I slip into high-alert mode, keenly aware I could tank or triumph. Flip a coin, it could go either way. Heads: security. Tails: insecurity. Security; insecurity. I understand my social insecurity's source, which stems from my young adolescence where some bullying events wormed into the stuff of my soil and planted some potently dark seeds.

Before jumping more deeply into this lagoon, I do want to say that I've experienced so much progress and redemption through coming face-to-face with God's healing power, through professional counseling and the Word He brings to life (and life in the things He does). I've had many a woman-at-the-well type of encounter with Jesus. Whenever I rub up against what used to be a bruise that no longer actively aches, I whisper a hearty *amen* for the places where the Great Physician has healed. He has gently planted me into more secure territory, which is what I'd like to talk about for the next few chapters.

Examining Roots

To begin my securing process, I had to look squarely at the root and "fruit" of insecurity, no matter how deeply I thought I understood it. Looking honestly was paramount. As I've mentioned, I've learned that insecurity and pride are often different sides of the same coin. Pride declares, "I am something." Insecurity demurs, "I am nothing." Self is the preeminent source of both, though one bent is more socially palatable than the other. Again, please hear me: I am not saying that this somewhat simplistic understanding of insecurity, in and of itself, is an antidote to the poison of insecurity. But, for me, it was a beginning, because if I can put words to it, I can begin to undo it. If I can name it, I can frame it. (With Jesus, of course.)

As I began to understand and define *insecurity* freshly, I understood there was, with Christ, a much deeper work to do and a much deeper work to allow. And as with all things, Jesus goes to the root. He looks to the source of the issue, the reality of the problem. I often imagine Jesus diagnosing the soil, and if the soil cannot support life, He graciously transplants that tree into soil that is good.

Let's peruse Psalm 92:12–14:

> The righteous will flourish like a palm tree,
> they will grow like a cedar of Lebanon;
> planted in the house of the LORD,
> they will flourish in the courts of our God.
> They will still bear fruit in old age,
> they will stay fresh and green.

Notice where the righteous person is planted and flourishing: the "house of the LORD" and the "courts of our God." The courts of the Lord were the courtyards of the temple, which at that time were as close as a man not in the priesthood could come to the Lord's presence. When the psalmist said the righteous are "planted" in the house of the Lord, scholars unpack that this word "planted" can mean planted or transplanted.[3] What a beautiful picture of the righteous being gathered and transplanted in the very house of God.

As I sit writing, I am watching my husband through the window, working in the yard on a cloudy day. My Tall Man is transplanting several large perennials (one being a persnickety, deeply rooted aster) to a new location in our backyard. We need to move it to new soil. At regular intervals, he comes into the house, collapses like a spent balloon, and catches his breath, chugging down water like a football player before he returns to the final, exhausting quarter.

If you recognize yourself in his physical exhaustion, then you understand the delicate care and strenuous work of moving a living thing from one set of circumstances and planting it in another set. The roots ought to be handled with kid gloves. Today, Jonathan isn't just throwing the shovel in the soil willy-nilly. He is doing this unseen work thoroughly and carefully so as not to damage the bush. Additionally, when you take out a plant or tree, you carefully inspect the roots.

Years ago a master gardener described to me the process of transplanting a bush and used it as an illustration for beautiful biblical truths. As she pulled out a plant from its tub, she said the first thing to do is make certain the roots aren't root-bound. This happens when a potted plant doesn't have enough room to spread out its root system, so the plant intertwines on itself, having nowhere else to go. As the roots take up more space than the soil, nutrients cannot be absorbed. When a gardener discovers a root-bound plant, it's essential to transplant it where it has room to spread out and grow.

Likewise, the Scripture is saying in Psalm 92, in essence, that God moves the beautiful cedar out if its native soil, and trasplants it into His soil—which is the courts of the Lord. Even the foreign tree—the cedar of Lebanon—will thrive and flourish in God's house. Jesus translates us from one set of circumstances to another, one set of "soils" to another, from the kingdom of darkness to the kingdom of light. Psalm 92 reminds me that flourishing in every season is living close to the presence of the Lord and His people.

Intimacy with Him. Community with others. These two set points of the heart are essential to begin moving from a life of insecurity to one of great security.

For my journey to security I had to take a long hard look at the "roots" in my life: Were they "planted by streams of water," as Psalm 1:3 encourages, or were they stuck in desiccated and nutrient-poor soil? In what, in whom, or where had I rooted my identity? As I could feel the Lord digging around the taproots of my life, would I surrender to the process, or would I fight Him on it? It seems ridiculous for a tree to fight the Master Gardener (just as it was ridiculous for the pot to argue with the potter in Jeremiah), but so often we do, clinging to old soil, old ways of being, old modalities of "mattering," and all the while the Lord is saying, *Surrender to the process. Let Me do My work. Let Me move you to a more spacious place. Let Me make certain the roots of your life are secure in healthy soil—rooted in Me.*

All this leads me to a Concealed Character from the third chapter of Joshua, as the people of God are finally, finally crossing into the land of promise:

CONCEALED CHARACTERS
A Priest's Burden During Israel's Crossing Over

I thought our flesh would wear through to bone. The weight of the ark of the covenant had often been as heavy as the gold that overlaid it, but that day it was a double weight that required a triple strength. I uttered a fervent prayer over myself—over each of the three priests. If we were to hold, we were to hold as a band, together, devoted. If one of us stumbled, we all would fall.

I called upon the strength of the ages and the Ageless One, whose covering had guided us through the wandering desert, whose beneficence had finally granted us a home. We were to stand for the people's passing over to the land of the promise.

My robes and sandals sank in the mud as I muttered Moses' last blessing over us as the descendants of Levi. That Levi would be blessed and accepted—this he prayed for us. I can still hear Moses' voice, on the edge of the land of promise, the shaking tones of authority and of acquiescence, in equal parts. The great prophet knew he would not enter the land. Moses had been called to lead us to it, but *into* it? This was Joshua's great commission.

Here, finally, finally and forever, was the day of crossing over. Crossing into.

It was so like and unlike the Red Sea crossing of our ancestors. This miracle was unusual, singular. As we stepped into the river, the waters recoiled. We four stood in the middle of the riverbed, in the place where the water had once been deepest. In the middle, the miracle materialized. Hundreds of thousands and more, crossing over on dry land while the river's roaring waters piled up at Adam. The men, women, and children were careful to give the ark of the presence, the mercy seat, wide berth. Some looked anxious to move toward Jericho, some seemed hungry to devour the fruit of the land, and still others were dazed from the years when our sandals had not worn out but sometimes our hearts had. Most looked ahead. Onward. Forward. Past the past to the future that awaited.

But some looked aside at us, taking in the weight on our shoulders and the length of time we stood. From some came quiet calls of "thank you," like the cooing of children, banishing the moment when exhaustion crawled across our faces. Stand and stand and stand. Stand again, in the next moment and the next and the next. In these times I remembered the contents that we held within the ark, the history which secured us as we stood. Words. Food. Branches.

We stood upon the strength hidden within.

Anchoring in the Hidden Place

For more than ten years I've been fascinated with the story this chapter's Concealed Character is part of—the story of the Israelites' crossing into the promised land under the new leadership of Joshua. I've always wondered about the way the priests, who were very human, understood their place in God's new chapter for His chosen people.

God began the narrative with Joshua by saying, "Moses my servant is dead. Now then, you and all these people, get ready to cross the Jordan River into the land I am about to give to them—to the Israelites" (Joshua 1:2).

After forty years of wandering in the desert, waiting for an unfaithful generation to pass the way of the earth, the season of promised-land living had come at last. God issued a call to action and specific instructions—they'd have to fight scores of resisters, cross a river that was flooding, and transport precious cargo, the ark of the covenant. When the people saw the priests who carried the ark of the covenant moving out, they were to take up their positions and follow along behind the ark at a specified distance. They were being led in a functionally new way, one they had not known before.

In my own life, when the Lord is doing a new thing (like moving me from insecurity to security), He often does it in a new way. For example, rather than allowing me to retreat into a cave of insecurity, He might lead me to places where my insecurity is brought into the light and can no longer be hidden. (As in, on the stage. As in, social settings where I feel supremely awkward. As in, tables at which I wonder why I am seated.) Talk about exposure therapy! For me it feels counterintuitive to deal with insecurity in the places where I would feel most insecure—*Lord, can we do this in private, please, and then step out, healed and whole?*—but there goes God, doing things in a new way. Showing me that He is with me in those very shaky, sometimes public moments. And there, with my arm in Jesus' arm, I risk the first faltering step of faith and not sight, knowing that though *new* can be disconcerting and uncomfortable, this movement is often the pathway to maturity and transformation.

That is exactly what was happening with Joshua at the Jordan River. As Moses' aide, Joshua had witnessed the Red Sea split—the old way of miraculously crossing a body of water: Moses held high his staff, the sea waters rolled back, and *then* the people crossed over. Here, the priests stepped into the flooding water, the water parted and piled up, and *then* the people crossed over. God was going to do a new thing in a new way.

So Joshua instructed the people to consecrate themselves

because the Lord was going to perform wonders among them the next day (3:5). Think of taking a really long shower before a big event—a wedding, a graduation, an interview. No hidden dirt or grime. This was a spiritual shower, of sorts. The next day, the priests began to move out toward the flooded river, and God's Word records for us that as soon as the priests' feet touched the water, while they were carrying the ark, the water "piled up in a heap a great distance away" (v. 16), and the entire nation crossed over on dry land.

Those priests, carrying the ark of the covenant, were commanded to stand in the middle of that riverbed until every person had passed by. I love the scripture that says the Levites "stood firmly on dry ground" (v. 17 ESV) until the whole nation passed over on dry land. Talk about "when you have done all to stand, stand then." This was a committed, substantive, and immovable crew, and they served faithfully, securely, in a hidden place. And, surely, it cost them.

I often wonder how long it took for every Israelite to make their crossing—how many days? Weeks? What a test of patience and endurance. Did the priests ever look at the entire nation plodding past them, feeling the weight of glory (acacia wood overlaid with gold *and* God's dwelling place) on their shoulders, and wish for just a moment to be one of the crowd going on ahead? Can you imagine how their muscles must have ached, or the caution with which they had to handle the ark of the presence? Maybe some felt fear rise as the sound of roaring waters piled up in a heap beside.

Of course, Scripture doesn't tell us their thoughts, but it doesn't stop a woman from wondering, and we do know from biblical history that the priests of God were as human as anyone else. I've always thought that the priests are the unsung heroes of this new-chapter narrative in Israel's history. It's tempting to look at them and think, *Yes, but they're priests; of course they stood faithfully. They were specially called to it, and they were made for it.*

We are, too, though. First Peter says, "You are . . . a royal priesthood" (2:9) and, in Christ, there is something of their spiritual mettle running through our veins. Their strength sings volumes to me across the ages, especially when I need to root myself—when I need to take a spiritual stand, as it were, against insecurity. I believe there are lessons of special resonance to glean from this chapter in the priests' lives.

Aside from faithfully holding the ark of the covenant, which represented the tangible presence of God on earth (Exodus 25:22), I wonder if the priests' faithful strength and security during a tenuous passage in Israel's history were sourced, at least in part, by the knowledge of *what* they were holding on to in the hidden place—the contents inside the ark. Maybe it's time to crack our own spiritual "arks" and see the ageless treasures hidden within. When our spiritual muscles are fatiguing, and our hopes are flagging, let's ask God for grace enough to remove the cover, because maybe, just maybe, we will find something hidden within that will give us something solid to stand on.

Words

Imagine the cover coming off the ark. Imagine the shadows fleeing, the light pouring in, and then . . . you see them. The stone tablets of the Law, the Ten Commandments, "the testimony" (Exodus 40:20 ESV). God's guidelines. God's very words.

It is easy for me, especially when insecurity is as unrelenting as the sea's ebb and flow, to become spiritually spun, to lose my bearing, to forget where I find goodness. I can become a bit scripturally anhedonic, losing my delight for those spiritual things that ought to be a source of joy.

Have you ever felt that way? So pushed and pulled by the currents of insecurity that even Scripture loses its sweetness? Where spiritual taste buds can no longer "taste and see that the LORD is good" (Psalm 34:8)? With all transparency, when I'm struggling with insecurity, the life-giving discipline of reading Scripture is often among the first disciplines that go. I seem to forget that the written Word links me to the living Word who is the transformative Word.

But it is then—it is *most* then—that I must return to the table and feed myself on food that cannot spoil, that cannot turn rancid, that only brings life.

Food

What other elements inside the ark were securing those priests in strength (and can help us when we wrestle with wavering insecurity)? Nestled next to those tablets was a simple bowl containing a sample of manna—those sweet flakes that came down from heaven when the Israelites couldn't feed themselves for eons in the desert. Years back, in my book about the desert experience called *Thirsty for More*, I wrote extensively about the consistent delivery of manna. Below are a couple of paragraphs from that work that apply to this discussion:

> Many Christians today equate manna with the reading of Scripture, and while that is certainly manna the likes of which we cannot survive without, I wonder if doing so puts too limited a definition to the word *manna*. Technically, manna is whatever physical sustenance God provides daily. Now, obviously,

the Bible spiritually fulfills this definition. We can (and should) open God's narrative daily and allow it to feed our very souls. Prayer is communicative, relational manna. Daily exchange with our Maker prepares us to face the hurdles and hurrahs of every day. These are daily mannas, and their importance cannot be overstated.

When I was in [a difficult] season, I had to ask God, aside from prayer and Scripture, "What is it? What is my manna, God? [The word *manna* means, "what is it?"] What are you providing as I sit here on the couch barely able to move . . . ? What's going to get me through this, Jesus? What is my manna—my food—in this particular desert? What comes daily from your hand? What is it? This supernatural experience . . . requires your supernatural provision. Give me the bread of heaven—that I have never known, that I will gather daily, and that I trust will come again in the morning hours. This is the provision I know I have never tasted. I will be looking for it each and every morning."[4]

At that time, I was looking for enough manna to get me through a difficult bedrest experience. Now I look to His manna to nourish me for the spiritual battle with my own insecurity. I rehearse (which means "to repeat") the truth of who He says I am. Memorialize the truth. Write it down. Pray it. Ingest it, daily.

A Branch

The ark holds yet another precious object. Not an everyday walking stick but a rod of sorts, perhaps knobby or arrow-straight. Contained within is Aaron's rod that budded at God's command (Numbers 17:8).

A group of Levites named the Korahites (we'll chat about that cohort more in a moment) rose up against Moses and Aaron as leaders, in an unholy kerfuffle regarding the priesthood. In addition to this rebellion, there was an outbreak of grumbling among the Israelites, and God dealt with it seriously—as in, deadly seriously. Peruse Numbers 16 and 17 if you would like to dive into this difficult story. In a nutshell, the Lord decided to settle once and for all who He had ordained to lead the priesthood *and* from which tribe. God instructed the Israelites to choose a stick for each leader of the twelve tribes of Israel and write the leader's moniker on it. Reuben. Judah. Asher. Levi. I bet you can imagine the snapshot. After this, they were to leave these twelve labeled sticks overnight in front of the ark of the covenant. The Lord said, "The staff belonging to the man I choose will sprout" (17:5). Scripture records what happened the next morning: "Aaron's staff, which represented the tribe of Levi, had not only sprouted but had budded, blossomed and produced almonds" (v. 8).

I'm not sure I can rightly express what this does for my often storm-tossed heart. I so often whisper prayers like, "Lord, just a little strength in this battle with insecurity is all I need. Just a little help, a little evidence of Your hand. Just a little." But this is a God whose resources never crater; His answers never falter. I all too often find my affections are too small and fickle. I think, *Lord, I'd be okay with just a little bud,* but He's never doing just one thing. In the biblical account, God took the branch from bud to blossom to fruit. Overnight. Not only was Aaron's once-dead-now-blossoming stick a reminder that God speaks dead things to life; it is a foreshadowing of Jesus' resurrection.[5] This hidden symbol also offers two significant anchor points for our security: our chosenness and our fruitfulness in God Himself.

Most of us, at some point in our lives, doubt our chosenness. Not necessarily out of self-pity (although it certainly can be), but often because the broken earth on which we live reinforces the fact that we may or may not be chosen—according to its preferences, distinctives, and whims. We wonder if our voice counts or our stories matter, especially when space is not granted.

As a kid, I moved a good bit, and one of the events that caused the most dread was the lunchroom. I can still almost feel the greenish plastic tray in my shaky hands; I remember the fraught scanning of the room, looking for a space or a friendly face willing to make one. I recall the practiced smile covering the hopeless exclusion. These moments didn't last forever, but they lasted long enough to leave my heart with scar tissue that still tugs and aches from time to time. So many of us are still in the lunchroom emotionally, hoping someone might scooch over and invite us to sit down. We carry these heart bruises into the here and now, so when we see others being chosen, included, or asked to come in close when we are not, we can begin to doubt our desirableness and, sometimes, our very worth.

Do you ever belt out the same tenuous tune? When I do, I need to pause for a moment and heed the rests. The rests in the music tell you when not to sing; they give you a place to catch your breath and prepare for what comes next. Aside from the fact that rests make the music as much as any notes do, they give us places to pause, to reset, to stop. Rests give us rest. And when we rest, here is what we might hear:

Child, it's okay to cut yourself loose from the culture's definition of worth.

Child, when you think you are still alone in the lunchroom, I am with you.

Child, I will always make room for you at My table.

Child, remember that My choosing of you means you can never be unchosen.

Again, I must lean into the meaning (and promise) of Aaron's budding rod: in Christ, we are chosen, and we will bear fruit. This is what the miracle meant to those priests: they stood, serving, because God had chosen them. Friend, you stand, serving, because God has chosen you. And your work, in God, will bear much fruit.

I cannot help but hear a foreshadowing of Jesus' words in John 15:16 in all this: "You did not choose me, but I chose you and appointed you so that you might go and bear fruit—fruit that will last." Friend, in Christ, the seeds you plant will bloom. In Christ, your life will bear fruit—and not just any fruit but fruit with a deliciously long shelf life.

All of that and more was hidden in the ark of the covenant. And it can secure us to the core.

When old-timey sailors were trying to make up time or pick up speed, they would sometimes cut weight or let go of unnecessary cargo weighing down the ship, making the ship lighter and faster. Since we've been imagining peering into God's holy ark, would you join me one more time for a "sanctified" imagination exercise?

Imagine looking over the decks of your life's ship. What is weighing you down? What is rotting? What rusted anchor keeps you from moving nimbly through the waves? What has God scrawled "OLD THING" on that needs to be hurled overboard? Maybe you can write the name of it now; scribble it right here in the margin. For me, it is faithless fear and outgrown insecurity. Tomorrow it might be something different. But for today, those two spiritual stowaways have weighed me down long enough, and they must go. Drowned in the waves of grace.

Hidden Memorials

When Joshua asked the men to take substantial stones from the middle of the river and make a memorial on the shore of Gilgal (their destination), he said the rock cairn would "serve as a sign among you. In the future, when your children ask you, 'What do these stones mean?' tell them that the flow of the Jordan was cut off before the ark of the covenant of the LORD. . . . These stones are to be a memorial to the people of Israel forever" (Joshua 4:6–7). The places God has brought us through are testimonies of His faithfulness.

When I first saw this years back, I almost wept. I have always believed that Scripture indicates another hidden memorial, built only by Joshua himself, in verse 9—a memorial not commanded by God as the Gilgal memorial was. Verse 9 tells the tale of Joshua's devotion and worship and remembrance in these astonishing words: "Joshua set up the twelve stones that had been in the middle of the Jordan at the spot where the priests who carried the ark of the covenant had stood. And they are there to this day."

In searching for a possible reason for this underwater memorial, I discovered this from commentator Donald K. Campbell:

> Joshua joined these men on their strange mission, and while they were wrenching up great stones from the bed of the river, he set another pile of 12 stones (NIV marg.) in the riverbed itself to mark the precise spot where the priests stood with the ark of the

covenant. This was apparently done on Joshua's own initiative and expressed his desire to have a personal reminder of God's faithfulness at the very beginning of the Conquest of Canaan.[6]

Friend, can't you see Joshua—a man with a head full of gray hair, a former and faithful "number two"—now being tasked with leading the nation, pushing twelve stones on top of one another in the middle of that riverbed, looking at the tired and cold feet of the Levites, knowing that as soon as God gave the command and they all moved on to take the promised land, the river would cover the secret memorial—rarely, if ever, to be seen by human eyes? This memorial is personal, private, hidden.

I desire a heart that memorializes, that marks, that takes time to remember what I am so apt to forget. We must constantly be reminded. We must constantly remind ourselves. Isaiah 46:9–10 calls us to do this holy putting back together or remembering of God's holy works:

> "Remember what happened long ago,
> for I am God, and there is no other;
> I am God, and no one is like me.
> I declare the end from the beginning,
> and from long ago what is not yet done,
> saying: my plan will take place,
> and I will do all my will." (CSB)

This settles my heart. There is a glory to the hidden life. There is a radical transformation when intimacy is pursued and cherished.

Joshua knew then what we hopefully know now or have remembered if we had forgotten it: the battle is won in the hidden places, in the hard in-between, in the long center years between the call and the fulfillment, in the difficult and faith-filled standing in the muddy riverbed, knowing that God is faithful and "an ever-present help in trouble" (Psalm 46:1). Joshua likely knew that every other promised land miracle, the taking of Jericho, and everything else that would follow were possible only because of obedience in the hard hidden season.

What is done in the hidden place will remain. And remain.

This spring I got to stand underneath those remaining Outer Banks oaks once again. Their cool beauty and gnarled glory spoke to me across the ages. How long have they stood, secured by ancient roots, sunk deep in the hidden place? Sunk deep, standing still.

May I pray for you?

Oh lovely, unceasing, unflappable Jesus, I cradle the heart of a friend—one I do not know by name, but You most certainly do. You have seen the hidden tears, the worship when all the lights go out, the shaky standing against all odds, the turned cheek, the love offered and unreturned, the clinging faith, the meekness in fury's face, the giving when there is but a nickel left, the weary heart petitioning the Source of Hope.

Jesus, You see the hidden memorials dedicated to Your grace. You see.

May these acts of quiet allegiance root the heart, mind, and spirit of the one for whom I pray. Your written Word, instructing; Your holy bread, sustaining; the bud and fruit of resurrection, resurrecting. May these three realities all secure this sojourn and sojourner, so that forward steps may be sturdier than ever before. After the public crossing, after the private memorializing, with the promised land materializing, lead my sister, lead my brother, all the way on. There is still so much good ahead. So much adventure to join You in. Because You do all things well.

Thank You, Great Water Parter.

CHAPTER 8

Anchored Community

Better is one day in your courts
than a thousand elsewhere.

PSALM 84:10

S everal years back, my husband was invited to lead worship with
a Christian ministry on a Caribbean cruise. Our RSVP was
"yes and amen," and how fast can we put on a Dramamine patch?
To my delight, the cruise offered an excursion to do something I'd
secretly wished to do all my life: swim with dolphins. *Flipper* reruns
at my grandmother Cleola's house had planted the desire to "dolphin" from an early age. I quickly signed up for it and was pinching
myself as I rode a bus to the compound where I would live out the
dream of a lifetime.

Now, as you have already read copious times in this book, I am tall. And because of said height, I've always had difficulties finding an appropriate bathing suit; they always seem to lack a certain *length*, causing them to ride up in all the very wrong places. For me, a bikini was already out, and so was a one-piece (again, not enough fabric). So I settled on a black tankini, which is what I was wearing as I waded into the water toward my great dolphin adventure.

I proceeded to hold on to the dolphin as instructed, ready to be one with the smartest mammals of the ocean. Without warning, the dolphin darted off like a bullet from a gun—and off went my tankini bottoms, which I caught by quickly bending my knees. So, yes, underneath the waterline, I was completely exposed.

All I could think was, *I am about to flat-out lose my witness as the worship leader's wife. And these poor people, who simply dreamed of swimming with the dolphins, are going to have nightmares of a stranger's posterior for the rest of the cruise.*

Y'all, there is a picture of me ripping through the water, appearing to be screaming with delight. I confess to you now that it was actually sheer terror. I am pleased to say, I kept anyone from knowing, as I pretended to be so overcome with emotion, sitting down in the water, shaking my head, as I repositioned my bathing suit.

I honestly walked away from that swim with a whole new respect for dolphins. All comedic insanity aside, these magnificent creatures have taught me some potent spiritual lessons. One of which is associated with their communal nature.

Sometimes they're with numerous others, sometimes only a few, but rarely are they alone. One article reports that only about ninety cases of solitary dolphins have been reported and studied.[1] Another states that scientists believe this solitary life could be a response to trauma.[2] This unusual "aloneness" makes them more vulnerable to injury and death. It's neither natural nor beneficial.

Oh, but when these beauties are together, they seem delighted to be alive: playing, communicating, and even, on occasion, surfing the waves.[3] Life—for them, and certainly for us—is in the *together*.

There are joys in being peas in a "pod." There is safety. There is the very real sense that, when we are together, we can be truly seen, strengthened, and transformed.

A Common Chorus

In the middle of your Scriptures, there is a hymnal of sorts, a book of song lyrics that the people of God sang to express their deepest desires, their greatest grappling, their fiercest fears, their powerful praise. These songs were sung in all kinds of settings—before battles, on pilgrimages to festivals, in corporate worship. These songs give us the language and music of the heart.

When you have run out of words for what you are facing, I promise you someone in the Psalms is singing them for you. The Psalms have many writers—the most famous are King David and Asaph. But we also have the composers Moses, Solomon, Ethan, Heman, "anonymous," and my favorite songwriting collective: the Sons of Korah, who provide the melody of this chapter. Eleven psalms are attributed to this musical crew, who used images of longing and passion unlike almost anyone else:

- "As the deer pants for streams of water, so my soul pants for you, my God" (42:1).
- "God is our refuge and strength, an ever-present help in trouble. Therefore we will not fear, though the earth give way and the mountains fall into the heart of the sea, though its waters roar and foam and the mountains quake with their surging" (46:1–3).

The phrases "the living God" and "the LORD of hosts" (ESV) are often used in the Korahite psalms.

The Sons of Korah wrote with a first-love passion for God. Deer panting. Mountains falling. Waters roaring. Earth quaking. Theirs are the lyrics of intimacy and zeal for the things God loves: His house, the bride. And the preeminent musical hook they sing? A love song to God Himself. Of all the anthems this group composed, Psalm 84 is my personal number one: a song delighting in pilgrimage. Some scholars believe that Psalm 84 is a psalm of pilgrimage and was sung on the way up to the temple, as it refers to the temple itself and the blessed "pilgrimage" taken to get there.[4]

A few months ago, in Israel, I had the unspeakable honor of standing on the newly uncovered "Pilgrimage Road"—a road thousands of years old—that pilgrims used going up to the temple from the pools of cleansing. Its length and breadth would steal your breath.[5] When pilgrims traveled to the required festivals at the temple, they would have traversed the Pilgrimage Road. While there, I thought, *I want to lie down in the dust of these stones.* I couldn't help but hear the lyrics of Psalm 84 echoing through the chambers of my heart. I could almost see hundreds of thousands walking step by step up to the house of the Lord. Together.

If it's not too odd, I wonder if you might sink into the back of your chair or favorite coffee shop seat, and slowly, purposefully listen to the sojourner's symphony of Psalm 84. May these words help you catch wind of heaven's refrain.

> How lovely is your dwelling place,
> Lord Almighty!
> My soul yearns, even faints,
> for the courts of the Lord;
> my heart and my flesh cry out
> for the living God.
> Even the sparrow has found a home,
> and the swallow a nest for herself,
> where she may have her young—
> a place near your altar,
> Lord Almighty, my King and my God.
> Blessed are those who dwell in your house;
> they are ever praising you.
> Blessed are those whose strength is in you,
> whose hearts are set on pilgrimage.
> As they pass through the Valley of Baka,
> they make it a place of springs;
> the autumn rains also cover it with pools.
> They go from strength to strength,
> till each appears before God in Zion.
> Hear my prayer, Lord God Almighty;
> listen to me, God of Jacob.
> Look on our shield, O God;
> look with favor on your anointed one.
> Better is one day in your courts

than a thousand elsewhere;
I would rather be a doorkeeper in the house of my
    God
than dwell in the tents of the wicked.
For the LORD God is a sun and shield;
the LORD bestows favor and honor;
no good thing does he withhold
from those whose walk is blameless.
LORD Almighty,
blessed is the one who trusts in you. (vv. 1–12)

As you may have noticed, Psalm 84 is no child's ditty or tender lullaby; it's a full-throated power ballad. I am always struck by the words "those" and "they"—the communal nature of this song's lyrics. Though there is a singular heart cry at the beginning, the heartbeat of the melody in the middle is a song of "we," and it is written by a "we" collective, the Sons of Korah. (More about their story in a moment.)

We are made to be seen not only by God but, safely, by one another.

We are made to be seen not only by God but, safely, by one another. There is a terrible human bent toward isolation. This bent is reflected in the story of our beginning—our genesis—in what God named the first "not good" of the Bible: "It is not good for the man to be alone" (Genesis 2:18). It was not good for man to be alone then, and it is still not good now.

During a recent tumultuous and insecurity-inducing season, I was tempted to abandon the spiritual pod altogether. I am not speaking of my faith—that root remained intact—but I felt tempted to abandon community. I am, by nature, an introvert in life and an extrovert onstage, needing loads of open time to be able to join Jesus in my calling to communicate the gospel. So I tend toward solitude even when everything is good, and more so during seasons of difficulty or fear. At the time, isolation felt safer. And in some ways it might have been, but it was not better.

During this bleak time in my life, a small bevy of friends quickly recognized my disappearing tendencies and flatly refused to allow me to give in to them. I cannot overstate the gift these friends were. We had copious conversations so complex it would take another book to parse them. They prayed (with or without me), offered Scripture touch points, asked questions, heard answers, and invited me to join them. And even when I refused, my ferocious friends would not accept my refusal. They saw when a "dolphin," made for community, was peeling off to solitary waters.

These come-alongsiders helped give my wounds air, soothed my weariness with words, offered hope when my sails were flagging. They saw me in the dust and spoke resurrection. They came to me in my own Adullam cave, drawing me into daylight and repeatedly reassuring me, proving themselves to be worth the trusting. They saw me, and in their seeing of me, I began to heal. In their seeing of me, I was affirmed. For this, and for them, I could sing a million praises and write a million psalms.

Friend, if you are in a season of struggle, I want you to know that God means for you to be seen by Him and by His people. Much of the anchoring of your heart will come when someone who possesses the heart of the Father looks at you and sees you with delight, compassion, and eyes that light up when you enter the room. Eyes that lovingly help you unpack deep complexities and journey with you to the only One capable of doing anything substantive about them. Eyes that delight in the unique expression of the imago Dei you are. Eyes that see this and journey with you toward a hopeful future.

You don't need many sets of eyes. You might even start by asking Jesus to provide you with just one *someone* with whom you can build a bridge of trust. (Once, back in 1994, I sent a written note over a pew to a friendly-looking girl in church, asking if she would want to get coffee sometime. I knew no one in the new city. Thankfully, Lisa said yes and remains one of my closest friends to this day.) It takes time, even in a physical sense, to build a bridge. Give the process of building friendship your patience and tenacity. Ask God for wisdom for the "next step" of friendship.

Being safely seen in community roots us in Him, *and* we get to be a part of bravely seeing others, which is a reciprocal gift. We become the person someone else needs and usually find the person we need in the process. We are seen by God. We see others. We are seen. In both the seeing and being seen, we are secured.

If your trust is flagging, perhaps your person, for a season, is a Christian counselor. Personally, I wish I had started my counseling journey sooner; the healing and wisdom it has brought to me is hard to articulate and would be even harder to live without.

And if I may: I encourage you not to forsake Jesus' bride, the church. If you've experienced church hurt (and, really, who among us hasn't?), ask Jesus for the wisdom to do the work necessary for righting the spiritual ship and, when the time comes, the courage to raise the sails again. Ask Him for a safe place to dip your toes back into the water. The local church can be beautiful, but it can also be messy and broken. Because . . . people. Still, I cling to the truth that we are living stones being built up as a spiritual house. Some of those stones are rounded and beautiful. Some are chipped and ragged. But Jesus, the Master Builder, uses them (us) all, crafting something that embodies and reflects the glory of the community of God. "He is making all things new!" Even our communities. Friend, it will not be the same without your voice, trust me. The bride's wedding gown may have some tears and stains, but, oh, how beloved she is by the Bridegroom. His death and rising is His vow to her, and He will not forsake her.

All this brings me back around to the Sons of Korah and a bit of their story's prelude, including their difficulties, their damages, their daring do-overs, and their delighted service to, for, and with the people of God.

A Contented Community

As we consider the themes of being hidden with Christ in God and being safely seen in community, one subject deserves special emphasis, and that is contentment.

The Sons of Korah gave us clues on how to court contentment in community. That sense of spiritual satisfaction is found in the words: "I would rather be a doorkeeper in the house of my God than dwell in the tents of the wicked" (Psalm 84:10). These are well-known lyrics if you've hung out in certain Christian circles for any amount of time. But how might they reflect the discipline of grateful contentment in God's household?

A quick backstory: During the days of Moses, Israel's tabernacle (a portable house of worship) was moved from place to place as the people of God wandered in the wilderness. Because of this, it had to be torn down and set up over and over again. If you've ever been a part of a church-plant meeting in a temporary home, you understand the set up/tear down circuit.

Kohath (Korah's grandfather) and his brothers, who were descendants of Levi, helped move the tabernacle; each one was assigned an implement to take care of. Kohath was responsible for physically caring for the ark, the lampstands, and other items. While his brothers got to transport their implements in carts, Kohath and his crew had a tougher task of carrying their items by hand, as God had commanded.

Is it possible that this greater difficulty in assignment planted seeds of discontentment among Kohath's team? If I were on their team, would I have thought, *Why are the other guys able to use a cart? Why is their job so. Much. Easier?*

Ever secretly harbored this thought? Ever wish you had someone else's story in the house of God? *I wish I had their gifting, calling, or level of worldly visibility.* Envy and competition can have a corrosive effect on our souls and on others' souls. They rob us of a million valued treasures, generosity among them.

Here's a truth I have learned the hard way: whenever I've been tempted to want someone else's calling, place, or visibility, *I know* that if I stood in that place, I would not have God's provision for that place because He has not called me to it. His provision couples with His vision. His enabling power and grace align with His will for us. The older I get, the more I find peace, security, and contentment in this: if God is not in it, I truly don't want it.

If God is not in it, I truly don't want it.

Ultimately, only contentment—a deep settledness in the goodness of God—can make us the kind of people who are joyfully secured in whatever adventure Jesus has called us to: small or grand, seen by many or unseen by all. This shift sets us free to want what we have rather than wanting what we "have not." What an absolute relief!

Let's check back in on Kohath's family, generations later. By this time in the scriptural story—Korah, Kohath's grandson, had been eaten up with some deeply bitter and entitled feelings.

Eventually Korah and his company rebelled against Aaron and Moses, challenging them for the priesthood and, ostensibly, the standing that went along with it. By this time, there could be no doubt about the corrosive effect of arrogance and discontentment, whatever their original source (generational or otherwise) may have been.

There was a problem, however—the priesthood was not something that was Moses' or Aaron's to give. It was God's. And because of that truth, a smackdown of the highest order occurred, in which God settled once and for all who had been chosen to lead. The earth opened up, swallowing Korah's crew and their tents into a crack in the earth (Numbers 16:31–32). The tents of the wicked went down into the earth. Do those "tents of the wicked" sound familiar? As in Psalm 84:10 familiar?

Now, there is an interesting thing about the mercy of the Lord. Apparently, a couple of Korah's sons survived (26:11). Perhaps they were too young to understand the whole unholy hullabaloo. The next time we hear of them, the family line was serving as doorkeepers or gatekeepers in the house of the Lord, as they said of themselves in Psalm 84:10. Let's touch base with this concealed character in Scripture, a son of Korah.

CONCEALED CHARACTERS
A Son of Korah

Keeping open the doors of the house of the Lord—let this be my assignment every day for the rest of my life. My relatives and my family were rescued from the tents of the wicked. This is why we name ourselves after the one who fell—Korah—but we also name ourselves as sons, a common unity remembering that God is not mocked, yet He left sons alive. The line of Korah did not die out.

God's justice ran as deep as a crevice in the earth, and His mercy ran as high as the Jordan River during flood season. The majesty of Yahweh's justice equaled the kindness of His mercy. Though rebellion seeped like septic blood through our family line, we were spared not just to swing wide the doors but to sing of the One who never ceases to swing wide the door for us. To join a joyful community. Oh, the great and wide mercy of the living God! Tomorrow, I shall wake and worship, again. In this I am fully content. For this reason, I will always sign my name as "Son of Korah." One of many. A thread in the tapestry. A word in a sentence.

I was at church a while back and asked the precious gentleman greeting people at the door how many years he had stood at that post, swinging wide the door for God's house, feeling content in his calling and purpose for that season, knowing he would never be widely known or visible, spending more energy seeing people than being seen. He grinned big as life and said it had been twelve years. A holy dozen. I knew he was going through a very trying season, and there he was every Sunday, not putting on a show but saying, "Let me hold open the door for you as you come to the only One who can help any of us through." I was challenged by his humility and thought, *What a modern-day son of Korah is he.*

Intimacy

A contented and close community where we are seen and affirmed, where we serve one another with joy and humility and a remembrance of God's great mercy, is also a place where we can cultivate a deep and serene intimacy with other fellow travelers and our Father.

Imagine you are a rural Israelite who has walked weeks to come to worship God at the temple in Jerusalem. You've gone from strength to strength until you appear before God in Zion, as Psalm 84:7 says. And after your long journey—finally, there it is. Maybe you've never seen it before. Maybe you've never seen it this close-up. The temple, the dwelling place of God, arrayed in all its splendor.

In many of the eaves and corners are birds' nests, and they are allowed to remain. The birds are so close. So intimate. And so messy. For many years I thought Psalm 84:3's reference to the birds' proximity to the altar of God was a symbolic way of expressing this sentiment: "I wish I were small enough to fly close to Your altar, Lord." Imagine my surprise when I read commentators who said the birds were quite real.[6] In some way, the swallows and sparrows got the best view in the world.

This beautiful avian reality was writ large on my very first trip to the promised land; as I was tucking my prayer into the Western Wall, I looked up—and what did I see? Birds nesting in the cracks and crevices. Imagine if you walked into church next Sunday and nesting birds were all over the ceiling. We'd be getting out our brooms and working to sweep those sparrows and swallows the heck out of dodge. But not so, our God. He doesn't swing brooms at them; He lays out the welcome mat. He allows them to remain.

Sparrows often represent insignificance; a pair sold for a mere penny. Jesus used sparrows as a picture of even the smallest things being seen by the Father: "Are not two sparrows sold for a penny? Yet not one of them will fall to the ground outside your Father's care" (Matthew 10:29).

Are you feeling invisible? Insignificant? Or maybe you feel overexposed and fearful? Fluttering about without a place to land? However you answer the question, you have an invitation: Come in close. Build your nest near the Father's altar. Your Father says you get the best seat in the house of God's goodness—the altar, where J. Alec Motyer wrote, "sinners are reconciled with a Holy God and He unto them."[7] Also a prefiguring sacrifice of Jesus, the altar is why you and I have the great invitation of intimacy with the living God the Sons of Korah were always singing about. Because of the once-and-for-all sacrifice of Jesus, we get to come in close.

About ten years ago when I was first beginning to dive into the song of Psalm 84, I wrote this short blog post:

It was a hot mess. And for the life of me I couldn't figure out why. (I am speaking about my front porch.) Every morning I opened my home's door to find it strewn with various bits of detritus. Chunks of Styrofoam. Bits of netting. Straggly sticks and stalks. By the end of the day said trash would disappear, which I chalked up to a good, stiff breeze. This mystery continued for several days until, finally, it dawned upon my toddler-addled brain to look up. And there it was—the beginnings of a nest. A really ugly nest.

Precariously perched in a small corner a mama bird was hard at work building a place to have her young. Her progress was not what one might call pristine or promising. Certainly not pretty. But she did not stop, and, eventually, she made something of a topsy-turvy home in which to lay her eggs.

I wondered what [folly] would cause a bird to build upon such a small, hidden eave, when anywhere else would have taken so much less work. Our front yard is full of perfectly good trees, ready-made for nest-building. However, I also saw that our neighborhood was full of mockingbirds, those aggressive birds that will dive-bomb the head of anything human, avian, or otherwise. This robin mama wasn't looking for pretty or easy. She was looking for protected, sturdy, safe. She was looking for close and hidden. And she was willing to do the awkward, messy work of creating that kind of home for her chicks.

All of this reminds me of Psalm 84:3, where the writer cries out: *Even the sparrow finds a home, and the swallow builds her nest and raises her young at a place near your altar.*

It strikes me that the bird (and the [anonymous Son of Korah] who wants to be like the bird) is desperate to build a nest near God's altar. Close. Tucked in. Intimate. And it amazes me that Psalm 84 says God welcomes the messy process of His people (like birds) bringing the bits and pieces of who they are, strewing the altar with the trash, because, well, because He'd rather have us close and messy than far away and pristine. Intimacy, like nest-building, is messy. But it is so well worth the mess. Especially when what you end up with is a nesting place nearer to God than you could have ever imagined. I've never wanted to be more bird-brained in all my life.[8]

And, might I add, I've also never wanted more to be like a son (or daughter) of Korah in all my life—content to be a part of the whole, a word in the sentence, a "we" and not just a "me," a living reminder of the beauty and bounty of a life hidden with Christ in God. Part of a glorious community: Contented. Intimate. Seen and secure.

Kindhearted Jesus,

I sit with You in this: being alone is often the bent of my heart.

I peel off from the safety of community because being seen in vulnerability is uncomfortable. I feel my spiritual arms cross and my heart pull away. I feel as if my lack and my shame will be the biggest presence in the room—if I even dare to enter the room. There is such risk in trusting, especially when trust has been shattered and is difficult to rebuild.

I say this, and yet I know to remain alone, apart, is not good for me, just as Adam's aloneness was not good for him. Help me heal. Help me trust You and live out the "one anothers" of Scripture You made me for. I want to carry and be carried; I want to pray and be prayed for; I want to know and be known.

Jesus, I lean into You as You walk into the rooms that I need to follow You into, so that I can become one of many. Amen.

CHAPTER 9

Holy Hide-and-Seek

I'll hide in the dark until night
comes to cover me over.
PSALM 139:11 (CEV)

The first year we went to the Outer Banks, the Cape Hatteras Lighthouse was being moved. Yes, *moved*. "Because of the threat of shoreline erosion, the Cape Hatteras Light Station, which consists of seven historic structures, was successfully relocated in 1999. The lighthouse was moved 2,900 feet from the spot on which it had stood since 1870. The entire light station was safely relocated to a new site where the historic buildings and cisterns were placed in relationship to each other exactly as they had been at the original site."[1]

153

Some perspectives are worth continuing to move for.

It was quite a sight to watch such a tall beauty creep along the shoreline, headed for a new home. The Cape Hatteras Lighthouse is the tallest brick lighthouse in the country, and, believe me, it's a doozy to climb. Once, years ago, I was about halfway up an Outer Banks lighthouse and had to stop, dizzy and dog-tired. Eventually, after regaining my composure, I was able to continue, and I am so glad I did; I could see for maritime miles. Some perspectives are worth continuing to move for.

As beautiful as the view is from many of these vertically gifted structures, the reason for the height and number of lighthouses at the Outer Banks is sobering. The water off this part of the Outer Banks is called the Graveyard of the Atlantic due to its dangerous shoals and channels for seafaring vessels. It is estimated that some three thousand shipwrecks are out there somewhere.[2]

In fact, some archeologists believe that Blackbeard's ship (yes, *that* Blackbeard) is located a mile and a half off the coast of Beaufort, in the channels of water sometimes called the Southern Outer Banks or the Inner Banks.[3] I wonder, if those lighthouses had existed back in the day, how many of those vessels—and the valiant souls who sailed them—would have been saved from ruin. If only they had possessed a light to rescue them when they were so off course.

I think back on the moment I discovered the hidden black whelk, partially submerged and obscured in sand. My hands dug it out gently and washed it off carefully so as not to lose my grip on it. The shell's discovery felt a little like finding the definitive item in an ultimate-stakes scavenger hunt. As I type, the shell sits wrapped in a towel, a sheet of bubble wrap protecting it in a special drawer. Its discovery was that precious to me. Still is. And though I'm not running upstairs to retrieve my black whelk, I am turning it over and over again in my mind, looking at its beautiful contours and whorls.

Using this shell as an emotional compass, I have hoped to explore another facet of hiddenness, and this one, I admit, is the one I struggle with the most. We'll get into those seaweeds in just a moment, but before we do, let's look at our Concealed Character, who has taught, secured, and healed my heart in the hidden place in ways that are hard to adequately articulate.

CONCEALED CHARACTERS
Gideon (to his son)

Now that I am at my life's ending, son, I want you to remember my beginning. Our beginning.

I will speak baldly so that the remembering will be easier when I am gone from this place of dust and bone and war. During the worst of our times, I hid our food. Whenever the fear in my stomach's pit felt as if it would digest me from the inside out and I'd be reduced to nothingness, I hid.

I resented being occupied in an occupied land, where I could not withstand our people's oppressors, but it had been that way as long as I had memory and my people had memory. I lived as a nauseous, green seaman would, hearing the war cry and the thousands of warriors rushing in like the ocean's unrelenting

155

crest. Our brutal oppressors left nothing in their wake.

We could never rally under the bullies that surrounded us. We couldn't protect our wives, our children, or least of all ourselves, so we all hid. In caves. Under cliffs. Wherever we could, wondering if the God our ancestors spoke of had grown deaf or, worse, indifferent to our cries. I clawed for a sign of Him. Pled for evidence of Him. Begged for the scent and sound of Him. For seven years, countless days upon days, our lives were rounded by fear.

And then, imagine an ordinary terrified day like any other— when I was hiding food in a place where our people made drink for celebrations, now used to grind enough grain for bread. Imagine, if you even can, the angel of the Lord appearing and turning to me, a sack of trepidation, and saying, "The Lord is with you, mighty warrior."

I was finally discovered by God in a child's game of hide-and-seek. In that moment, I could hide no longer.

Maybe some of you have heard the story of Gideon, one of the judges who ruled Israel during a lawless, faithless time in Israel's history. Aside from Samson's story, Gideon takes up the most real estate in the book of Judges, so you might be wondering why we are looking at him as a Concealed Character. On the face of it, he's not very concealed. Maybe, like me, you learned his story of fleeces and shrinking armies in a neighborhood Vacation Bible

School or Sunday School puppet shows. Yet lately I've been looking at Gideon's story through a different lens, and it's brought a new insight into focus, one that strikes me to the core: *hiding and being hidden are not the same thing.*

Being hidden with Christ in God is a glorious invitation from God and a beautiful spiritual reality. But hiding is a human bent, a reaction to a myriad of things: pain, fear, overexposure, bullying, insecurity. In an emotional and spiritual sense, we often confuse one with the other, don't we? Left to our own devices, it's easy to take a beautiful blessing from God and turn it into a curse. For instance, humility *can become* self-humiliation. Discernment *can become* criticism. Mercy *can become* enabling. Pursuing hiddenness in Christ *can become* hiding away from the call of God on our lives.

> When the angel of the LORD appeared to Gideon, he said, "The LORD is with you, mighty warrior."
>
> "Pardon me, my lord," Gideon replied, "but if the LORD is with us, why has all this happened to us? Where are all his wonders that our ancestors told us about when they said, 'Did not the LORD bring us up out of Egypt?' But now the LORD has abandoned us and given us into the hand of Midian."
>
> The LORD turned to him and said, "Go in the strength you have and save Israel out of Midian's hand. Am I not sending you?"
>
> "Pardon me, my lord," Gideon replied, "but how can I save Israel? My clan is the weakest in Manasseh, and I am the least in my family." (Judges 6:12–15)

First off, I grin when I read "Pardon me, my Lord."
Second, I wince to hear my own heart's contents so aptly

expressed in Gideon's response to the angel's command, saying, "No, Lord, I am the least of the least. The weakest of the weak. I am a speck of dirt on a wad of gum on the dirty sole of a shoe." Anyone else hear their heart here too? Hello, pain. Hello, deflection. Hello, *overidentification with defeat and insecurity.*

Still, the Lord is relentless in His assurance of Gideon. "I will be with you, and you shall strike the Midianites as one man" (v. 16 ESV). Commanding the hiding man to come out of his "cave," God's messenger called Gideon to believe that His presence makes anything possible. Anything. Even facing down threatening bullies.

So how do we manage this, friend? How do we move from hiding to moving out into the great adventure of being hidden in Christ *and becoming free*—free to step into anything, anywhere, anytime with Jesus' umbrella over our heads?

While this holy story contains many amazing tips, let's take a fresh gander at a few.

Your Father's Turning

There is little in Gideon's story that slays me more than this phrase: "The LORD turned to him" (Judges 6:14). But before we unpack the emotional core of that truth, I wonder if you might meander off the beaten beach path with me for just a moment or two.

In Scripture, when God turns His face away or hides His face (a form of turning away), it is almost exclusively a result of sin. If you search the Bible for the phrases "turn my face away" or "hide my face," most instances concern God turning away from His people due to sin.[4] A holy God cannot look upon sin. Deuteronomy 32:20 puts it this way: "'I will hide my face from them,' he said, 'and see what their end will be; for they are a perverse generation, children who are unfaithful."

What are we to do—we, who so feel the depth of our own sin? Our great remedy is found in Christ, who paid the ultimate price for sin, even enduring His heavenly Father's forsaking of Him. The apostle Paul said of Jesus' sacrifice on the cross, "God made him who had no sin to be sin for us, so that in him we might become the righteousness of God" (2 Corinthians 5:21). Because of Jesus' eternally efficacious sacrifice, God never turns away from us but rather toward us, for all eternity.

Even prior to Jesus' crucifixion we see rare times when this beautiful, intimate reality of God's turning toward us comes into play. When Peter denied Jesus the third and final time, Luke noted, "The Lord turned and looked straight at Peter" (22:61). The Lord turned toward Peter, not away from Peter. And that turning caused Peter to weep over the battering betrayal he had visited upon Jesus; I'm quite sure seeing the face of the One who so loved him broke him. Talk about kindness leading to repentance.

And when we see another beautiful turning in the Old Testament, it is just as stunning. Jacob, after a brutal, all-night-long encounter of wrestling with the angel of the Lord, said, "I have seen the face of the Lord and yet lived to tell the tale" (my paraphrase). That is why he named the spot Peniel, which literally means "face of God" (Genesis 32:30).

When God turned toward a person in the Old Testament, it was momentous. It's striking that several of the times God's turning occurs in Scripture, it is in the midst of very fraught circumstances. Like Gideon's story in Judges 6. The God of all glory turned His very self to this terrified, hiding man. It's no different for you and me today.

> **When fear has us frozen, the Lord turns to us.**

When fear has us frozen, the Lord turns to us. When we are certain we can't possibly try again, the Lord turns to us. When we lose hope, the Lord turns to us. When the attacks won't abate, the Lord turns to us. Again, God always makes the first move. Friend, is there a place where you know you are hiding, where you know that Jesus is calling you to step out of the shadows? He is turning to you. You don't have to move first; you need only to respond to Him.

Your Father's Voice

After the Lord turned to Gideon, He said to him, "Go in the strength you have" (Judges 6:14). Go. I love the "gos" of Scripture, don't you? Somehow, they dislodge my stubborn stuckness. "Go . . . your faith has healed you" (Mark 10:52). "Go and learn what this means: 'I desire mercy, not sacrifice'" (Matthew 9:13). And, of course, the greatest "go" in all the Bible is what we call the Great Commission: "Go and make disciples of all nations, baptizing them in the name of the Father and of the Son and of the Holy Spirit, and teaching them to obey everything I have commanded you" (Matthew 28:19–20).

The word translated as "go" in the Hebrew means "go."[5] I love it when a word is so essential that it means . . . itself. In the New Testament the word "go" has a bit more shading to it: "Go" is taken from a Greek word that means passageway, travel, and, among other things, contains the sense of movement. Going from one place to another.[6] When I am stuck in a place of hiding, my heart is transformed by moving, not by standing still. You've probably heard Newton's first law, which says that a body in motion will stay in motion, and a body at rest will stay at rest, unless another force acts on it. I find the same to be true of myself when stuck.

When you know God is calling you out from hiding, ask God for the grace to move.

When you know God is calling you out from hiding, ask God for the grace to move. Just the next right move. Just the next step. Just the next prayer. Just the next.

Insecurity loves to leave you marooned on an island—because the longer we stay marooned, the harder it is for us to dive into the water or even to wave down the ship that has been sent for our rescue.

Maybe your first step is simply writing down where you sense God is leading you out of hiding. Maybe it's praying about that place with a trusted friend. For most of us, the first step is small, quiet, and graced. God's grace is especially present for our first step, just as a parent's grace is present for a toddler's first step. We see in Scripture that God graced Gideon's first steps, answering his cry for multiple miraculous signs of God's presence—all so Gideon would know that, even during his insecure circumstances, he was secure in the good Father who called him out.

When I recently was stuck in a season of hiding, I heard the internal whisper of the Lord: *I will hand-feed you.* I envisioned a small cardinal perched on the strong and sure hand of the Father, tipping in its beak, feeding on the seeds cupped in the hollow of His palm.

It was as if He was saying, *I am going to give you sustenance at every turn, but you must allow Me to do so. You won't have to work, but you will have to receive. My job is to provide; your job is to respond.* Every time I would see His miraculous provision or invitation, I would say yes and ingest. If I can put into words what those moments felt like, it was as if God was whispering, *I'm going to provide everything you need for this opportunity, but you must show up for it. I'm going to offer wisdom in the difficulty, but you must act upon it.* I would receive and respond. Eventually my wings began to find their strength once more, preparing to fly again into the great adventure with Jesus.

In Judges 6 the Lord called Gideon to move into a great adventure as well: to strike down the Midianites. Gideon protested, saying, in essence, "But You've abandoned us, Lord, so how can that be? We have no evidence of Your presence." Here, he revealed how little godly confidence was stored in his heart. His confession was rooted in fear, abandonment, and insecurity. He had, at least at the moment, lost his yes.

That God didn't dialogue with Gideon's fear is interesting to me. I'm not saying God didn't go to battle with Gideon's fear—He absolutely did by giving the mighty antidote to it, which is His very presence—but He didn't dialogue with Gideon about it. Sometimes I need to resist dialoguing so deeply with my fear and insecurity and instead begin dialoguing with the God who is over my fear and insecurity, attuning my ears to His life-giving, faith-inducing voice. Recently when struggling with a resurgent insecurity, I found myself rehearsing and rehashing the reasons for it. I put those reasons on repeat—and even when I didn't speak those reasons aloud, they were always on loop in my head. The constant dialogue with insecurity didn't do a thing to alleviate my stuck state. If anything, it reinforced it. So I began to dialogue with possibility, with hope, with the little bit of faith within.

God actually dialogued with the little bit of faith Gideon did have—the shadow of the brave man inside. He said something interesting: "Go in the strength you have and save Israel out of Midian's hand" (v. 14). At first glance, we might be tempted to think this was a call for Gideon to use what small measure of strength, what small self-confidence, he possessed. In other words, we might think God is saying something like, "It's okay, Gideon. I see that pitiful little bit of strength and confidence you have, and that'll be enough."

But I don't believe that is what this passage of Scripture is saying. Let's face it: Gideon didn't really have any strength of his own. I believe God was saying to him, "Go in the strength you don't yet know you have." Which is God's strength. It's an odd kind of strength; the kind the Bible says is made perfect in our weakness and, yes, friends, even in our insecurity. God said to Paul in 2 Corinthians 12:9, "My grace is sufficient for you, for My strength is made perfect in weakness" (NKJV). Did you notice the peculiar phrase "My strength is made perfect"?

God didn't say His strength is made a little bit better or a little stronger—no, He said it is made perfect, whole, complete, fully consummated even.[7] Right in the place of your deepest weakness. That's why Paul said in verse 9, "I will boast all the more gladly about my weaknesses, so that Christ's power may rest on me." What if our weakness was cause for worship rather than worry—especially in a culture bent toward strength and perfection?

Our culture tempts us to boast in strength and accomplishment, not to hold high our weakness or wounding. I have never once posted, "I am so grateful, so thankful that when I speak I feel like I am going to toss my cookies, because God's strength is going to be made perfect there. Drop a heart if you feel me." Now, I'm

> **Our weakness is a magnet for the perfect strength of Almighty God.**

not saying that posting that all the time would be a wise move, but my point is, we curate the highlights, the strengths, of our lives for public consumption, don't we? Yet it is our weakness, not our strength, that attracts God's strength. Our weakness is a magnet for the perfect strength of Almighty God. And for many of us, our weakness is in the place we are the most insecure, like Gideon was.

Why is this so often how the Lord works? I deeply believe it is so we can be living emblems of God's upside-down kingdom distinctive. Paul wrote:

> God's foolishness is wiser than human wisdom, and God's weakness is stronger than human strength. Brothers and sisters, consider your calling: Not many were wise from a human perspective, not many powerful, not many of noble birth. Instead, God has chosen what is foolish in the world to shame the wise, and God has chosen what is weak in the world to shame the strong. God has chosen what is insignificant and despised in the world—what is viewed as nothing—to bring to nothing what is viewed as something, so that no one may boast in his presence. (1 Corinthians 1:25–29 csb)

The longer I walk with Jesus, the more I believe with all my heart that He makes far more use of my consecrated weakness than He does of my so-called strengths. He's saying to you and to me, *Go in the strength you have that you don't fully know that you have—which is a bigger, more confident strength than you ever dared to dream—and I will help you navigate the storms of your fear and insecurity.*

Something that always fills my hope reservoir from Gideon's story is this: the battle's unusual strategy and endgame were opportunities for God to show His complete sovereign strength over circumstances and challenges.

The Israelite army was whittled down to a nub—they didn't have nearly enough brawny soldiers to face such a brute force. The final battle was not even a traditional war; it was decided by a cacophony of sound (pots beating

> **The longer I walk with Jesus, the more I believe with all my heart that He makes far more use of my consecrated weakness than He does of my so-called strengths.**

and trumpets blaring), and God, through these miraculous means, squarely won the day. And the war. It's astonishing. From invitation to initiation to consummation, the battle was God's. All Gideon needed to do was to begin to move against the current of insecurity, hold up his weakness to God's mighty strength, and step out—to take one obedient step after another.

I had a friend who once told me her heart resided on the back row of the church for years, as she chose not to use her gifts or follow her calling because of her insecurity. She was terrified to step out, even in a small way. Stuck. Hiding.

Eventually, she started to stretch her spiritual muscles, risking a bit, being willing to fail, and trying again. She was still a bit afraid, but with each new "go" she responded to, insecurity lost its power over her, and she started to re-engage with God's invitation to her much-afraid heart.

If you're in a terrified, stuck place right now, ask the Lord to guide you, like an Outer Banks lighthouse might, safely back to a secure harbor. Gently reinvest yourself in the truth that you are "hidden with Christ in God" (Colossians 3:3) no matter what enemy "should threaten to undo [you]," as the old hymn says.[8] The most essential part of who you are, if you have trusted Christ for your salvation, is already safe, secured, and covered in Him and His finished work at the cross. You have a strong Helper who "sits enthroned over the flood" (Psalm 29:10 ESV) and is constantly turning your "darkness into light" (18:28).

> Insecurity doesn't have the final say over your life; Jesus does. And in Him, you're going to make it—secure and safe and daring and bold.

Insecurity doesn't have the final say over your life; Jesus does. And in Him, you're going to make it—secure and safe and daring and bold.

Can you see it? His light is scattering the shadows. It is shining through the darkest night.

Life-giving Lord,

I admit here, before You, that there is a tender place where You are calling me out of hiding. What I have too long called safety has now become a place of stunting. My spiritual muscles are atrophied from too much cramped hiding. I want to dream again, Jesus.

To do this, would you breathe upon the coals of my heart as I begin to speak it out, to move again into the spaces of grace? Lord, there are enemies afoot. Sometimes I can sense them, sometimes I cannot. But You do, Lord, and the spiritual battle does not worry You. It is often, in fact, where You do Your best work.

So, Father, I'm leaning on Your everlasting arm. I'm stepping into the glorious light You offer Your children. I'm asking for the shadows in my life to scatter as I follow You into whatever is next.

Thank You for never abandoning my heart. Thank You for never leaving me alone in my hiding but tenaciously leading me to the ultimate hiding place. You. Yourself. Always and forever.

Free

PART 3

CHAPTER 10

Strong Sea Legs

God is within her, she will not fall.
PSALM 46:5

I perch at its edge. I ingest its glory.
I shrink in its waves. I awe at its story.
I cradle its gifts. I wonder at its withholding.
I breathe its life. I hurt for its home-goings.
The ocean's shifting. The ocean's immutability.
The ocean's familiarity. The ocean's incomprehensibility.
I am swaddled in its sound and found in its fury.
This is what it means to perch on the edge of the
    ocean.

Much research has been done regarding the awe factor. When we stand before something as gigantic as the Atlantic or the Grand Canyon, we understand how small we are. We realize that we are only a part. And rather than causing us to fold into infinitesimal nothingness, these moments create a positive feeling, one that actually increases great happiness.

I think often about Abraham gazing at the starry sky of promise (Genesis 15:5) or David penning, "The heavens declare the glory of God; the skies proclaim the work of his hands" (Psalm 19:1). Or Paul's beautiful scripture, which feels emblematic for our time together in this book: "Since the creation of the world God's invisible qualities—his eternal power and divine nature—have been clearly seen, being understood from what has been made" (Romans 1:20). When we see what God has made, we see His fingerprints. What is invisible is, somehow, made visible.

Something about the vastness of God's creation secures me in my place in it. If He can create *that*, He can take care of me. I look at the sky's inky color wheel and marvel, *You, oh Lord, breathed life into all of this. You, oh Lord, are the breath in my lungs as well.* I return again to the truth of Colossians 3:3: *I am hidden in the One in whom all spiritual blessings are hidden. I am seen and secured by the One who allows me to glimpse His glory.*

God allows Himself to be seen. We need only lift our eyes to His holy horizon.

God allows Himself to be seen. We need only lift our eyes to His holy horizon.

The Slump

I've always had problems standing up straight—physically and spiritually.

It's funny the memories that remain from a young life, some

wrinkled and fizzed by age, others as sharp as the bracing winds of the sea. From the time the first growth pains ached my hips and femurs, a curved posture has been the bent of things for me. I recall being on a junior varsity cheerleading squad (the miracle of making it remains a mystery). At the season's start, the skirt fell appropriately on my thighs. By the end of the year, the one remaining photo I have shows me head and shoulders above the other girls, with a skirt barely covering my posterior. I'd put on inches like the other girls put on Add-A-Beads. I was not quite as tall as a tree in that awkward braced-teeth shot, but I was well on my way. If I had a crisp twenty for every time a dance teacher instructed me to "stop slumping!" or I was asked about being a star basketball player due to my vaunted height, I'd be able to purchase that trip with my husband to Florence, Italy, that I'm always dreaming about!

Vivid are the memories of school dances, slumped over to try to lessen my height for the boys who asked me to slow dance. Vivid are the emotional snapshots of sinking into a hip, trying to look like whatever gaggle of girls I happened to inhabit. Vivid are the memories of "Wow, you're tall" before I could even spit out my name in an introduction. As pants became high waters within months and new shoes were discarded before being fully broken in, I innately understood it was important to shrink. I wanted to lessen whatever quality made me different—as if I was the check on the "none of the above" box.

This is what it's like to long to be anything other than what you are.

I started testing the waters of theatre during those young years. When I went to final callbacks, the need for slumping felt critical if I was going to have a shot of making the show. By this chapter of my story, I was taller than almost every guy. I once saw an old video of me in a show, and I spent every solo singing bent like a broken branch, trying to reduce myself to my scene partner's height. Even as I grew older, even though I had brilliant directors who utilized my gifts in roles where the height served the story, the slump had taken root—not just in my spine but, most destructively, in my soul. I tried desperately to be smaller than, to connect in a world where I was different. Add to my out-sized height some bizarre, socially ostracizing events, and you've got a disastrous recipe for a life of insecurity and flat-out terror. By the time I finished high school, I was six feet on the outside but minuscule inside.

I simply could not inhabit my stature. And I didn't want to.

When I went to conservatory for acting, the calls for me to stand up straight began immediately. In ballet, in acting, in move-ment, in combat, in mask work, and in speech, my stature was, if not in the spotlight, at least on the stage. The only time I was put on probation (common at the time in my conservatory) revolved around my physical inability in the more physical classes.

During my sophomore year, we were assigned an intensely preparative exercise that was based on watching an animal at the zoo and then humanizing and extrapolating the animalistic char-acteristics into improvisations and scenes. I remember wanting to utilize the giraffe, since I identified with its long neck, lumber-ing legs, rueful glances, gentle nature, and absolute oddity. But I refrained from choosing the giraffe, as I thought it might call too much attention to my height, and surely the professors would scoff at such an obvious choice. It was the kangaroo instead for me: scrunched up, hunched over, bouncing with its head down. Just one more example of how I simply could not inhabit who I was and how

I made significant choices that supported that deep-rooted lie and the pain that went along with it.

During this strange season, a mighty spiritual seed was planted. As I came running headlong back into the arms of Jesus and began the hidden, difficult, quiet work of facing who I was, who I had been, and, most importantly, who I was becoming in Christ, the seed started to break open, like a chrysalis, hidden and unseen, metamorphosing, transforming into something altogether different.

The metamorphosis from caterpillar to butterfly is such an interesting process, but one stage of the process has long fascinated me. After the majority of the transformation has occurred and just before the butterfly is about to emerge from a chrysalis as a flying beauty, a mighty struggle ensues. The butterfly begins to make its way out and to move its weak wings against the casing. This struggle is said to give the butterfly's wings the strength to fly. Often, it is the struggle that gives strength. Our struggles, in God's hands, likewise transform and conform us into His image, preparing us to fly. As is often the case, like the butterfly, we don't necessarily shed what or who we are; instead, we are transformed by the power and efficacy of His Word and His ways—after all, the caterpillar is still in the butterfly somewhere. So the transformation begins.

Often, it is the struggle that gives strength.

Day after day, as I spent time in His presence, in His Scripture, and with His people, my bent spine started to straighten out by degrees. Once, a friend had me do an exercise reading Psalm 139 aloud. Though exercises like that might be common enough now, back in the late 1980s, they were quite unusual. I looked at myself, still a bit slumped, all seventy-two inches, and was struck with awe: *Oh heavens, oh Jesus, it is You who knit me together in my mother's womb; You made my inmost being; You created me this way—every freckle, every wild curly hair, every foot, and every inch. All five feet, twelve inches. Brokenness and blight and beauty, all in a piece. You did not make me to spend my life with bowed shoulders and head, trying to cram myself physically, emotionally, and spiritually into a small, cramped box.*

The words oddly spoken over me at a Bible study years previous—ones I had carried around on yellowed paper for years—suddenly came flooding back: "God made you tall, Allison, like the cedar. He made you tall, and He is going to use what He made." In my young life, I had rejected those blessings because they confirmed something I was trying to hide from. I didn't want to be a cedar. To be a cedar was to stand out and be solitary, liable to be chopped down for firewood. To be seen in this way was unsafe.

Long, Tall Sally

Whenever I read the story about the bent woman in Scripture, her story rings like a tonic note in my soul:

On a Sabbath Jesus was teaching in one of the synagogues, and a woman was there who had been crippled by a spirit for eighteen years. She was bent over and could not straighten up at all. When Jesus saw her, he called her forward and said to her, "Woman, you are set free from your infirmity." Then he put his hands on her, and immediately she straightened up and praised God.

Indignant because Jesus had healed on the Sabbath, the synagogue leader said to the people, "There are six days for work. So come and be healed on those days, not on the Sabbath."

The Lord answered him, "You hypocrites! Doesn't each of you on the Sabbath untie your ox or donkey from the stall and lead it out to give it water? Then should not this woman, a daughter of Abraham, whom Satan has kept bound for eighteen long years, be set free on the Sabbath day from what bound her?"

When he said this, all his opponents were humiliated, but the people were delighted with all the wonderful things he was doing. (Luke 13:10–17)

So much leaps from the page: Jesus was busy, fully engaged in ministry. He was speaking in the synagogue. People were surely pressing in to hear the words of the ages roll from His holy tongue—yet, in the middle of a sermon, He stopped cold. Jesus interrupted Himself for a woman whose God-created body had been bent for eighteen years—approximately 6,570 days. We don't know whether she was born with the disability or struck with it later in life, but we do know her life must've been agonizing. An exercise in living on the periphery. A less-than life. And then . . . Jesus saw her.

I wonder what her internal monologue was during this encounter. I can only imagine.

CONCEALED CHARACTERS

The Bent Woman

Me? Me. He looks straight at me. His gaze does not turn away. And every eye turns with His. Glowering gazes. Brutal brows. The teacher means to make a mockery of me. To hold me up as an embodiment of the Almighty's displeasure. I know it is so, as it has ever been so.

I drop my eyes where they belong. Down. Down. Down. I should turn and go. The crowd will part Red Sea-like to let me pass—careful not to stand too close, and I can return to . . . to what? To what shall I return? To what have I ever returned? The tormentor's cruel lips, eyes that wait to look me over and judge me as a thing less than nothingness?

I can feel His gaze upon me. What compels me toward the melody of this man, I cannot say. I speak inside myself, *You can't . . . You mustn't . . . It isn't safe.*

Love. Fight. Victory. Vindication. I have never seen such things in another's eyes. Yet they are in His eyes. This man has the power of the gale and the fury of love in His eyes. Seeing me, He now calls me. "Come forward," He says.

Come forward.

I feel my feet moving, against hope. Each step is painful, but not as painful as the tongues clucking disgust as I pass by. I persist. With each footfall, I step closer to reach the One whose words shut up forever the voice of shame and batter bondages until they are dust. We have all heard the stories of children coming back from the grave, and those oppressed, as myself, being righted like a once-listing ship. We have all heard.

I reach Him, finally. I am too close to lift my eyes. His feet are my only vista.

And then He speaks: "Woman, you are set free from your infirmity."

Woman, seen. Woman, acknowledged. Woman, freed. Woman, healed.

As He speaks and lays His hands upon me, my spine obeys the One who commands the winds and the grave. My height grows back; inch by inch, like a bent stalk reaching to the sun, I rise. I struggle to stay on my feet, the center of me changed now. The unadulterated light near blinds me. But I adjust. It has been eons since I have seen the horizon, witnessed the circling birds, the tops of trees, the tops of heads. The view is so beautiful. My tears are my food; they fill my mouth as I mouth without sound: "It is all true. It is all true. You are all true."

I turn to go, never thinking such a gift could ever be mine.

The back of me still feels the weight of His hand. The miracle of my spine was far less than the miracle of His touch. The Enemy's final lies unbinding and unwinding. He acknowledges me. He calls me daughter of the promise. His words war with the curse I have ever and always lived under. I have no daughter. I am no daughter—Abraham would never claim me. The Teacher grafts me back into the family tree; He says I am a part of God's creation and shall never be cut off again. Their clucking tongues cannot do it. Their hatred cannot do it. Their self-righting cannot do it. No power of the earth can undo what He has done.

To be seen. To be healed. To be touched.

To see the bluest sky.

To unfurl.

179

To finally unfurl.

Oh, how I know what this is like. In my final year at school, I was cast as the lead in the musical *The Boys from Syracuse*. The character of Adriana was regal, emotional, and a bit wacky. As I stepped into her shoes, I somehow stepped fully into my own. I remember rehearsals in those halcyon days, the windows open in our rehearsal room in Margaret Morrison Carnegie Hall, letting in the first breaths of spring. Spring was on the way; something new was on the wind. And it was. Even when the other actors with whom I shared scenes came to my chin or shoulders, I stood, planted like a tree. Like a cedar after all. If I used my height in a physically comedic way, I did it on purpose, not because I was trying to hide in plain sight. It was delicious and new and utterly authentic. I found a confidence on that stage that had been years in the making . . . and, I believe, a real work of God's Spirit. The confidence spilled from the stage into real life, as I found myself embracing my full height. Standing up straight, finally. I still need a good reminding here and there, but I am so much more apt to pull my shoulders back and be who I was created to be.

I joke about my height a good bit when I have the grace-filled opportunity to speak to women at events and conferences, by introducing myself this way: "Hey, y'all. I'm Allison Allen; I'm a five-foot-twelve perimenopausal mother of a fifth grader, whom Jesus Christ absolutely ruined for the ordinary over a quarter of a century ago. That's my story, and I'm sticking to it." There are plenty of giggles to go around, but what strikes me most are the women at the book table afterward who lean forward and talk quietly to me—sometimes commiserating about their height, sometimes sharing that they, too, always felt on the outside, different, always trying to lessen their height, struggling to see it as an unusual gift from their heavenly Father. Tender to my heart are the teens, standing by their mothers, sunken into a hip, shoulders already slumped. I try to whisper into their ears that one day they will unfurl, too, and what makes them different will one day be used like a trophy of grace in Jesus' hands.

They need not fight to be seen, but they need not run from it if the sovereignty of God makes it so. Be as tall as you are.

Maybe it's not your height that makes you feel different or less than. Maybe it's social anxiety that steals your words when you enter a room. Or a physical difference that makes climbing stairs an exercise in exposure. Or a lack of resources in a school that is overflowing with them. Maybe it's high-functioning autism, trying to decipher social cues. Maybe it's the whispers of gossip and shame that echo around you in the dark watches of the night. Maybe, like the bent woman, it's the unrelenting back-riding of the Enemy, who tells you you will never belong, never be truly seen or free, that causes you to feel unseen. One of the only antidotes I know for this societal and adversarial poison is to consistently, almost violently, unhook from the world's ways of envisioning us.

Sometimes that means going all the way down the rabbit hole with Jesus, sitting with Him there at the rot-gut bottom that rocks the core of me, and letting Him speak through His Word to my heart. Meeting Him there, where terror and longing twist around me like the embrace of unholy twins. The bottom of my rabbit hole is this: I may never matter to those I wish to matter to. I may never be seen by those I wish would see me. My voice may never be the desired voice in the room. I may never be acknowledged in conversations I wish to participate in. My words may never have the reach I wish they would. I may never make the grade. As my grandmother Loreah would say, "No one can be everyone's cup of tea."

I have to sit with it for a moment. Maybe you do too.

It's okay. It won't kill us. By the power and presence of Jesus, the bottom of the rabbit hole won't undo us.

We may never matter in the way the world says we should. But the Spirit will bring us to places and spaces and communities where our words and hearts do matter, if we are willing to go with Him there. To trust again. I think we should sit with Jesus in those tender places. I think we should acknowledge the painful rubs and aching emotional bruises—because we gain nothing from running from true things, and because He is with us in them. In what is actually true.

Jesus has already perfectly walked this road. In fact, His lack of acknowledgment—His lack of "mattering" in the world's eyes— was foretold by the prophet Isaiah, and it was part of the prophetic checklist for the poor and powerless to recognize Him:

> He grew up before him like a tender shoot,
> and like a root out of dry ground.
> He had no beauty or majesty to attract us to him,
> nothing in his appearance that we should
> desire him.
> He was despised and rejected by mankind,
> a man of suffering, and familiar with pain.
> Like one from whom people hide their faces
> he was despised, and we held him in low esteem.
> Surely he took up our pain
> and bore our suffering,
> yet we considered him punished by God,
> stricken by him, and afflicted.
> But he was pierced for our transgressions,

he was crushed for our iniquities;

the punishment that brought us peace was on him,

and by his wounds we are healed.

We all, like sheep, have gone astray,

each of us has turned to our own way;

and the LORD has laid on him

the iniquity of us all. (Isaiah 53:2–6)

Known as the Suffering Servant prophecy, this chapter in Isaiah is the ultimate prophecy of the One who would come to redeem the world. Yet look at His LinkedIn profile: A dry root. No beauty. No majesty. Nothing to look at. Despised. Rejected. A suffering and pained man. Without esteem. Mistaken as God-cursed. Punished. Stricken. Afflicted.

Jesus was not only not feted or accepted or celebrated by the world, but He was patently rejected by it. Mark 8:31 says, "He then began to teach them that the Son of Man must suffer many things *and be rejected by the elders, the chief priests and the teachers of the law,* and that he must be killed and after three days rise again." Think about the crucifixion and resurrection that we stake our lives on. We identify with this great work; we talk about picking up our cross and carrying it daily (Luke 9:23). But I will never, ever forget the first time this scripture leaped off the page at me. Part of the prophetic fulfillment of the rejection forecasted in Isaiah 53 was that Jesus would be rejected by the religious elite (or those in power). At some tender point in our lives, it will not be any different for us. Someone we very much want to gain attention from will not give it. Someone we very much want to accept us will not. We may experience a painful rub where we are even patently rejected. Abandoned. Ridiculed, even. In the rocked reality of this place, what do we do?

Personally, I lean on Jesus' arm, and I allow the hurt.

Miraculously, I begin hurting with hope.

Slowly, I can identify God in the circumstances. *There it is: His wisdom, His care, His empathy.*

With His breath in my lungs, I begin to breathe again.

With His strength, I stand. I rise. I unfurl. And I remember that the world's rejection cannot undo me when the Father's acceptance has defined me.

Not-of-This-World Values

Jesus could not be affirmed by the world, at least in part because He was not of the world. As He talked with His disciples about His impending fulfillment of Isaiah's prophecy, Jesus proclaimed, "My kingdom is not of this world. If it were, my servants would fight to prevent my arrest by the Jewish leaders. But now my kingdom is from another place" (John 18:36). In other words, Jesus said His rule and reign is eternal—it's heavenly, it's forever, it's above, and it's mightier than the sword. Jesus knew He would soon sit at the right hand of the Father, in full authority, and His reign would never end. This is, in part, the rousing call from Colossians 3:3–4, writ large.

Additionally, Jesus had so much to say about our invisible, unseen, hidden life. Matthew 6 is a portion of Jesus' mountain-moving sermon called the Sermon on the Mount. Not only did Jesus exhibit a life of hidden intimacy and prayer during His ministry on earth, but He encouraged His followers (and us, as well) to follow the same principle.

Listen to some of these upending scriptures:

- "Be careful not to practice your righteousness in front of others to be seen by them. If you do, you will have no reward from your Father in heaven" (v. 1).
- "When you give to the needy, do not announce it with trumpets, as the hypocrites do in the synagogues and on the streets, to be honored by others" (v. 2).
- "When you give to the needy, do not let your left hand know what your right hand is doing, so that your giving may be in secret" (vv. 3–4).

Jesus went on to speak of prayer (v. 6) and fasting (v. 16) in the same mode. In our outer disciplines (giving), in our inner disciplines (fasting), and in our transformational disciplines (prayer), Jesus exhorted us to exercise them privately, intimately—in secret. Don't be gloomy when you fast, don't pray on the proverbial stage, and don't give with gongs ringing. Jesus assured us that our great God sees us in the secret and will reward us openly. (And I might add: the longer I've walked with Jesus, the less the public reward seems to matter.)

Personally, I'm not called upon to fight for an earthly kingdom (including my own). As I write, I have to remind myself of this, even today—and as I do, the temptation of placing my life's pilings too deeply in the soil of earth loses its appeal. And an astonishing reality begins to be revealed, like an unusual black whelk: whether I matter here matters so much less than being set free to run hard after the call of the King.

But here is the gloriously freeing truth as I grow older, and

> We matter to the One who matters—who sees us, secures us, and ultimately frees us—and that is more than enough.

maybe it will free you a little bit as well: we matter to the One who matters—who sees us, secures us, and ultimately frees us—and that is more than enough. We can allow ourselves to delight in the fact that no matter who may overlook us, our heavenly Father does not. Know that there are communities of His making where we can joyfully contribute and be safely seen. There are places and spaces that need what we, by His grace, offer. So allow Scripture to wash away the wounding of the world. Allow Jesus to combat the lies we have too long believed. Though none of it is easy, it is so worth it. And when we unfurl, when we become as tall as we really are, we are able to lift our eyes, set our minds, and run freely toward the One who makes all things new (Revelation 21:5).

Freedom Bringer,

I don't know how You do it, but You always do. You bring my freedom to me. Mercy and goodness. Following me, even when I stand on the outside. Even there, You see me; You secure me; You free me.

Today I ask for grace to receive Your healing, to heed the invitation to stand straight. To ride through the waves, knowing that You are the mast I am lashed to, and I will make it through. I will unfurl. I will follow.

And, Lord, please, make this freedom song resounding in my heart echo in someone else's. May my burgeoning places of healing and freedom become something that attracts others to You, like a holy siren song drawing people to Your healing. To Your Majesty. To your ever-seeing, ever-freeing pursuit.

As I unbend, I know I will never see the sun, the earth, the sea, and this life the same way. Thank You.

CHAPTER 11

An Unknown Freedom

He came to Jesus at night.
JOHN 3:2

There is a different kind of dark on the Outer Banks beaches. There are no boardwalk lights or blinding developments flood-lighting the shores. At night, the canopy can be as opaque as ink. Or it can resemble a heavenly chandelier, made by a million pin-points of light. Or an endless tapestry of tar. It all depends on the stars.

Nighttime navigation is not for the faint of heart. Particularly before the advent of radar and GPS and accurate water-depth maps, sailing at night was an audaciously brave person's game. If the night was cloudless and clear, the map consisted of stars. The biggest "sky marks" were lodestars like Polaris or the larger constellations. I bet there were midnights when the sailors thanked "the Father of the heavenly lights" (James 1:17) for a single star.

There are times when I have stood on the dunes of the Banks at night and recalled so many dark nights of the soul—and so many lodestars that popped out at my soul's midnight. I think of those moments where my ability to see was obscured, but—there in the night—Jesus was waiting, if only I could move toward Him.

I've always been intrigued by those spaces, and how, when we move in faith to and through them, we find a supernatural freedom. In 2011, I wrote a piece that was one of my first Concealed Characters, though I wouldn't have termed it as such back then. I imagined a world in which key characters from Jesus' life would have gathered to eulogize Him, since after that *first* Good Friday they weren't yet aware of Resurrection Sunday. The piece is called *Requiem*. Though we know this character by name, still, I wondered about Nicodemus and how Israel's teacher might have parsed his own dark night of the soul when the Messiah was gone. Here, I imagine him speaking to Mary, the mother of Jesus.

CONCEALED CHARACTERS

Nicodemus (to Mary)

I was there. In the tomb. In the end.

I came to Him first in the dark of night. The night was stingy with its stars. Our council had gone long that day, hashing out a grave and disastrous concern. A concern that could be—and would be, many swore—the undoing, the unseating of us all.

His name, Jesus, had been spoken before, but on that starless night, His name was followed by curses and spitting as the reports grew more and more hideous to some but intriguing to me: dead girls rising, blind men seeing, kingdoms coming. His words, even when repeated through the grinding teeth of the high priest, bore life. Even secondhand, His words midwifed hope in my precise and careful heart.

So I sought Him that starless night, afraid to be seen near Him. When I knocked, He opened His door, smiled, and invited me in. I don't know why I expected anything else. Face-to-face we sat, and words spilled out.

I started. "Rabbi, we know that You are a teacher come from God, for no one can do these signs that You do unless God is with him."

He didn't reply to my greeting but said something I still think on: "Truly, truly I say to you, unless one is born again he cannot see the kingdom of God."

"How can a man be born when he is old?" Of course I spoke of myself. "Can he enter a second time into his mother's womb and be born?"

Jesus answered, "Truly, truly I say to you, unless one is born of water and the Spirit, he cannot enter the kingdom of God. That which is born of the flesh is flesh, and that which is born of the Spirit is spirit. Do not marvel that I said to you, 'You must be born again.'"

You must not marvel, Nicodemus. Jesus knew I was marveling.

He called me the teacher of Israel, yet, in all my life, I had never spoken words as true as His. I carried His words with me back out into the night. And the starless dark seemed like light to me because of His words.

When what was done to Him was done, when the sacred voice that had spoken such words spoke no longer and the body was pierced to prove the deed done, I traveled with Him. Joseph, from the town of Arimathea, had purchased a virgin tomb, and we laid Him in it—hundreds of pounds of myrrh were bought to perfume it. The scent of death was not meant for Him, so I scented the air. I did not know how else to show my love for Him.

I, who once came for His words in the dead of night, buried Him in the light of day. Instantly, I knew I would forever be identified with the Carpenter and His words because of this. My name, I know it, will never again be spoken of without the name Jesus in the same breath. As it should be.

Joseph and I wrapped Him as gently as a babe, I promise you, Mary. And I confess to you today without shame that I spoke His words back to Him there. The words He had said to me on that starless night.

"For God so loved the world that He gave You—I know You were speaking of Yourself—that whoever—even a religious man with a careful heart—believes in You shall not perish but have eternal life."

Such words. I do not know how to live in a world without such words.[1]

The Unknown Space

We assume the story didn't stay in a painful place for Nicodemus, because we know the resurrection is coming. But at this point in his story, Nicodemus didn't know that. There was so much he couldn't wrap his head around. He was in the transitional in-between.

Once, reflecting on the liminal space between the first Good Friday and the first Resurrection Sunday, I wrote a poem called "The Great In-Between: A Good Friday Reflection." I've felt it a time or a million. Maybe you find yourself there now. If you do, please know that the Lord stands with you in that tension.

> When what matters most seems marred—
> When shame won't loosen its chokehold—
> When the summit you must take is ice-slick—
> When hope has hidden more treasures from you
>   than it has revealed—
> When all would be well if you could just get to
>   sleep—
> When doors slam tight, and windows don't open in
>   their stead—
> When you'd give your last dime for some
>   good news—
> When the miracle you crave comes neither fast
>   nor slow—
> When the ol' college try nets you more of the same
>   ol' same ol'—
> When waiting loses its wonder—
> When loneliness won't leave you alone—

When you are certain that death will always have
    the final say—
Pause.
Pause for just a moment.
And ponder a possibility.
The possibility that, perhaps, you're living in
    the Great In-Between—that fraught space
    between Promise and Fulfillment. Between
    Waiting and Wonder. Between Death and
    Life. Between Friday and Sunday.
Have patience for that place because it will not last
    forever.
A rally will rise. A cry will be answered.
Today, you may find yourself between the agony of
    Good Friday and the rebirth of Resurrection
    Sunday, but remember this: though what
    you're walking through may feel like death
    itself, the day of Living Again is sneaking up
    on you.
Remember the Great In-Between.[2]

How are we transformed in the in-between spaces? These transitional spaces are the spaces that allow us to come face-to-face with the God we hope exists. The One who meets us in our darkness because He has overcome our darkness. Who transforms our darkness because He has triumphed over it. As the psalmist wrote, "Even the darkness will not be dark to you; the night will shine like the day, for darkness is as light to you" (139:12).

We cannot know this God without this journey into the in-between. It is the in-between that proves it to us. Who is this good

God who invites us to wrap our lives—body, soul, and mind—around the promise of His presence and anchor our very lives, our sanity, around the pylon of His grace?

We serve a God who sees around corners. We serve a God who knows the unknowns.

> **We serve a God who sees around corners. We serve a God who knows the unknowns.**

One-Name Wonders

Iddo. Junia. Sheerah. Asenath. Jochebed. Priscilla. Zipporah. Aquila. Archippus. Apphia. Onesimus. Nympha. Epaphras.

So many of the phrases I've circled in my Bible contain a name. A single name—sometimes with a sentence of explanation, and sometimes these monikers fly solo. Names containing mostly unknown stories and glories, these secondary and tertiary characters in God's epic love story nestle into the folds of my brain and circle around there.

Did Asenath, daughter of the pagan priest of On and wife of Jacob's son Joseph, have any inkling of her status as the mother of the two half tribes of Ephraim and Manasseh, and the outsized part they would play in God's story? Did she know that Ephraim and Manasseh would replace Reuben as the firstborn of the nation? Did she know that Jewish children would be blessed with the words "May God make you like Ephraim and Manasseh" (Genesis 48:20) still today? Did she understand her rare position as an outsider grafted into the family tree of God's people?

Which prophecies caused Iddo's hands to shake as he recorded

God's words and warnings during the reign of Solomon and Jeroboam? Where are his words now?

What kind of city builder was Sheerah? Did she draw up ancient architectural plans?

What kingdom exploits did Nympha participate in?

I truly think on these and so many other names. Perhaps because I have generally played lesser-seen characters onstage and been an understudy, I find these parenthetical people particularly intriguing. In college we were often assigned the task of researching secondary characters, filling in the societal and cultural blanks, deciphering what their motivation might be for their onstage actions, words, and feelings. We tried to ferret out what the author intended to say through these characters. Though this is a far, far lesser metaphor for the same pursuit in the biblical narrative, I think this has always been the source of my bent to lean toward the unknowns, the hidden characters in the pages of Scripture.

God knows every unknown.

That word *unknown* used to cause my heart to pinch up a bit; how about yours? I'm a word girl to the marrow, but I don't like this word. The word *unknown* makes me turn my head away. Unknown things, at least for me, feel shadowy, slightly dangerous, apt to wrap themselves like anchors around my legs and drown me.

Once, while I was visiting with a wise woman at my collegiate church, I received something that forever encapsulated my tendency toward hating the unknowns. After praying and talking with me, she said something akin to, "Allison, I imagine you as a young girl, presented with a beautifully wrapped present from your heavenly Father. But you won't unwrap it because you're afraid it contains snakes. But it doesn't. It contains untold blessings. You stand frozen, looking at it, refusing to unwrap it. Unwrap the present."

Sometimes I'm still tempted to believe that blessings always come with a billy club. But it's not true. Scripture declares, "The blessing of the LORD enriches, and He adds no sorrow to it" (Proverbs 10:22 BSB). Slowly, the emotional fog is lifting; I dare to raise a new sail. Yesterday, my Tall Man and I were talking about the things we can't see (the unknowns), and he said something powerful to me: "You've spent your whole life thinking if you can't see it, it must be all bad. But what if you can't see it, and it's all good?"

I thought: *I don't have to know every loop-de-loop, because God does.*

Up and Up and Up

Recently, my family went on a trip to the mountains of North Carolina, and I thought it would be a dandy idea to walk across the Mile High Swinging Bridge at Grandfather Mountain, America's highest footbridge. I thought I would lollygag right on across the bridge with plenty of cute family selfies to boot. How high and mighty of me!

I got to the edge of the bridge, started to take the first step, and then accidentally looked down. I pulled back to the platform of safety like a woman who had just been asked to do a triple gainer off a high dive into a pool of molten lava. I was terrified, which was odd to me because I had never, in all my life, struggled with heights—but that day, there was no way I was going to make it across that bridge without adult diapers.

Once I had caught my breath, I looked at my husband, my two sons, and countless others walking calmly across the bridge. After glancing at the safety wires going up to the neck of the bridge, I told myself, *You can do it; just don't look down.* I looked at the destination and the objects of my affection—my husband and my sons (Levi, named for the priests, and Luke, a tip-of-the-hat to the beloved doctor of one of the Gospels)—the whole way across. I looked at where I was going and, step by careful step, I traversed it. And heavens, what a view was waiting for me on the other end!

The key to the whole experience was found in looking up, not down to the gorge below. The key was setting my mind on higher things. I could not help but think of Jesus, who set His heart and mind on the joy set before Him as He endured the unendurable.

In Plain Sight

After the crucifixion and resurrection of Jesus, there was a boatload of confusion among those who had followed and loved Him, as well as among those who were on the periphery of His ministry and teaching. Scripture is clear that His followers didn't understand that Jesus would rise from the dead.

But even those who didn't recognize Him as Messiah would've heard about (and possibly witnessed) some sea changes in Jerusalem: an earthquake, darkness at midday, and the temple's thick curtain torn from top to bottom. Bodies bounded up from their graves, women reported seeing angels and the missing body of Jesus . . . the list goes on. So much to process. So much to make sense of.

At the following point in the postresurrection story, we find two disciples who were agitated by recent events and befuddled that Jesus had not delivered to the Jewish people an earthly kingdom as they had expected:

Two of them were on their way to a village called Emmaus, which was about seven miles from Jerusalem. Together they were discussing everything that had taken place. And while they were discussing and arguing, Jesus himself came near and began to walk along with them. But they were prevented from recognizing him. Then he asked them, "What is this dispute that you're having with each other as you are walking?" And they stopped walking and looked discouraged.

The one named Cleopas answered him, "Are you the only visitor in Jerusalem who doesn't know the things that happened there in these days?"

"What things?" he asked them.

So they said to him, "The things concerning Jesus of Nazareth, who was a prophet powerful in action and speech before God and all the people, and how our chief priests and leaders handed him over to be sentenced to death, and they crucified him. But we were hoping that he was the one who was about to redeem Israel. Besides all this, it's the third day since these things happened. Moreover, some women from our group astounded us. They arrived early at the tomb, and when they didn't find his body, they came and reported that they had seen a vision of angels who said he was alive. Some of those who were with us went to the tomb and found it just as the women had said, but they didn't see him." (Luke 24:13–24 CSB)

There are so many things about this passage that grab me and make me grin at the same time, if only because I see myself so deeply in them. First, we can't gloss over the fact that the Emmaus disciples' lives had been flattened in an emotional hurricane. All their hopes about Jesus—and how He might deliver them from

Roman rule—had been smashed to smithereens. In addition, some of their women were telling strange tales about a missing body and resurrection. They were walking through (and arguing about) a tragedy, conundrum, and mystery.

Into this spiritual tangle, "Jesus himself came near and began to walk along *with* them" (v. 15 csb). There He is again. With. But even with the Savior walking alongside them, curious about their arguments, explaining all things about Himself in the Scriptures, "their eyes were kept from recognizing him" (v. 16 esv).

> **Even when we can't quite recognize Him, Jesus still comes in close, walking alongside us, patiently and perfectly revealing Himself to us.**

(An aside, if I may: even when we can't quite recognize Him, Jesus still comes in close, walking alongside us, patiently and perfectly revealing Himself to us.)

It was not until Jesus took the bread, blessed it, broke it, and gave it to Cleopas and the unnamed disciple—an action I imagine would have been a reminder of the Last Supper—that Scripture records "their eyes were opened, and they recognized him" (v. 31 esv).

Friend, they had been walking with Jesus, but He had been hidden from them in plain sight. How many times when we feel bereft is His arm encircling our waist and holding us up? How often have I missed His beautiful visage because it was veiled by distressing circumstances? How many times have I averted my eyes from Him because I didn't understand the tumult of what had just happened?

Once the Emmaus disciples saw Jesus, their hearts began to

burn within them. After such an encounter, they *knew*. They recognized Him for who He actually is—not a ruler who had come to overthrow earthly kingdoms but a suffering King who would overthrow death, hell, and the grave once and for all. They were citizens and recipients of a kingdom hidden from human eyes but embodied and seen in the risen Christ.

Just as Paul reminded the Colossian believers, there is no hidden, secret knowledge but only a revealed Christ in whom we, as people of faith, are all hidden.

He Knows, So We Don't Have To

Years ago, when my husband and I thought we were called to be contemporary Christian music artists, we formed a duo called allentown. (Our name was a reference to a Billy Joel song. We thought the lowercase *a* was particularly edgy, but I digress.) We had had some small success, receiving a favorable review in *CCM* magazine (back when physical magazines existed), performing a smattering of regional concerts, taking tons of label meetings, and experiencing so many "almosts." There were so many unknowns, so much wondering how God desired to use us. We spent so much time in the in-between.

During this season, we wrote these words:

> *I don't have to know.*
> *I don't have to know.*
> *Whether you move me fast or take me slow,*
> *I don't have to know.*
> *All the answers and where you'll take me.*
> *All the answers just might break me.*[3]

These lyrics were our attempt to capture the truth of Jeremiah 29:11–13—not just that we don't have to worry about the future, but we don't even have to know it. In fact, sometimes the knowledge wouldn't be good for us.

Though these words were the cry of my late-twenties heart trying to resist wresting back some control, there's something about this heart cry that invites me to a simpler way of approaching life. When the path before me is obscured by a dark sky, there is a hand to grasp. When the directions I have are inscrutable, there is a voice to heed. I can trust and follow, trust and follow, even as only one next step is revealed at a time.

For me, life transitions are times when I feel particularly vulnerable, when I am most prone to make grabs for control and try to force particular outcomes. But I've learned it is wise to resist that urge. It even mirrors the process of childbirth: during the transition phase, the body is making more room for the baby to be born. If you push at that time, you can actually cause the structure to swell and make the baby's birth more difficult.[4] The baby will come into the world, to be sure, but there is a right time to push, to join that work, and that time is not when the body is in transition. When in transition, don't push.

This preaches to me in the spiritual realm. When in the transitional in-between, it requires more faith to allow the process to play out, waiting upon the Lord, than to strain and push for something to happen when the time simply isn't right.

This sentiment of surrendering to God's schedule is seen throughout Scripture. In Habakkuk 2, for example, God assured the prophet that He would carry out His will in His perfect timing and led him into waiting: "The vision awaits its appointed time. . . .

If it seems slow, wait for it; it will surely come; it will not delay" (v. 3 ESV).

Wait for it; it will surely come.

Y'all, this call to self-restraint strengthens me in the waiting rooms of my spiritual life. It's the inspiration I need to avoid pushing and shoving and rushing, because I know I can trust Him.

Following the All-Knowing God

When I give in to this surrender, it's such an enormous relief. I can trust Him enough to simply *rest*. I don't have to manufacture a result or figure out what's coming—because He does. And He's so good.

I get to follow a known God into the unknown.

I get to follow a God who knows me and knows every unknown I will ever face.

What power these words hold! They can loosen the tight coil of anxiety. Quiet the storms in a heart. Set a soul free from struggle.

I can think of no other so-called god who ever allowed such intimate access to its presence. Who allowed such careful religious men, like Nicodemus, to come visit in the dead of night and spoke to them there the world's most upending words. Who knew before He ever suffered on the cross that His followers would be gutted and raw, oblivious to the coming resurrection. Who walks with us in the night season and, because of His immovable proximity, transforms us into more deeply trusting creatures. Who is this One who knows, who lets us come close? The Lord. The Almighty. The Maker of heaven and earth.

He is also the One who *leads*.

"The LORD himself goes before you and will be with you," we read in Deuteronomy 31:8. "He will never leave you nor forsake you. Do not be afraid; do not be discouraged."

The God of the universe goes first.

The Lay of the Land

When I go to an unfamiliar setting—a gathering, a party, an event—I want my Tall Man to go first into the room. Always have. It makes me feel protected in some way. I know I can lean into his presence. I can trust his lay of the land (or "lay of the room," as the case may be). For years he has tried to get me to go ahead of him, knowing it to be the polite and southern thing to do, but I insist on following him. I follow closely, but I follow, nonetheless. I follow him, because the truth is that when I go first, I feel shaky, and when he goes first, I feel secure.

Multiply that security exponentially when it comes to following God's lead.

You never have to go first into any situation you face. When you walk into that doctor's office to get those results, God goes first. When you sit down with your child's principal, God goes first. When the text comes that you've been dreading, God goes first. When you're presenting that business idea, God goes first. When you send your baby to pre-K, God goes first.

Whatever we face—good or bad, monumental or minute— God goes first.

His knowledge and foreknowledge transform my careful and concerned heart. Miraculously, I feel freedom's flag unfurling inside. There is no room He asks me to enter that He hasn't already walked into. There's no corner that He doesn't see around. There's no injury or incapacity in us that He hasn't combed through, and still, He says—as He said to Peter—"You! Follow Me!"

This. Sets. Me. Free.

We follow a God who gets there first.

Friend, I so deeply want this rest and freedom for you too. I gently encourage you: start to open your heart to this, to the One who offers it to us.

I know it's not easy. Maybe you've stepped back from the story God is writing, feeling bound by the things you cannot speak aloud. The self-inflicted wounds, the stubborn wanderings, the disappointments in others, the choices that have crippled. You might be afraid to trust again—yourself or anyone else. But even that can't change the reality that when you can't see what's in front of you, God is still at work. No matter how you're feeling, He is so powerful and so unreservedly for you. He knows your every wound, your every flaw, your every tendency, and still He reaches to you, this very moment, inviting you into His great story.

Come, take a new step with me.

Jesus,

I confess that I'm carrying the weight of unknowable out-comes. I'm ruminating over "what ifs" and "what nows." I'm operating like everything rests on my shoulders.

My mind leans toward fear, not faith. The mov-ies I play out in my head often don't end well—because I'm imagining stories without You in them.

I try to force outcomes, to control and overwork and manipulate. And I'm tired. Tired of taking on a job that is not mine. Tired of living in a world that doesn't exist yet.

And so, I pause. Jesus, help. Jesus, help me to see this self-focus for what it is: a sin-bent reliance on self, a preoccupation with fear, a refusal to trust Your wisdom.

I confess. I turn. I remember.

I receive Your fierce kindness in this tender place. Breathing on the coals of trust. Cradling my oh-so-human heart in Your capable hands. Impressing upon my soul this sentiment: The future is too much for you, child; it is Mine. All that will be is Mine. All that will be is already in My safekeeping.

Jesus, by Your goodness, I trust.

CHAPTER 12

Treasure Hunt

It is for freedom that Christ has set us free.

GALATIANS 5:1

It felt like a bibliophile's treasure hunt every time I went in.

For years there was an old Outer Banks bookstore that was a hidden gem. I discovered it quite by accident in 1998, during the first rainy spate I experienced on my first visit to Kill Devil Hills. The sea poured from above and below. I was freshly married to my husband, Jonathan, who couldn't swing the time off from his new job. Missing him to the bone, I timed my phone calls (let us have a moment of silence for the corded phone, please) to when he would arrive home to our little apartment. My hand—and heart—felt empty as I strolled the beach, wearing a hooded jacket, pelted by drizzle and the occasional bit of sea foam.

I longed for something to fill time's void on those days without him. One day, I happened upon the bookstore, nestled ingloriously in a nondescript strip mall. I wish someone would make a scratch-and-sniff patch for the scent of a musty bookstore at the beach: dampened paper, salty air, long-ago-smoked cigars, moldering cardboard boxes, a tinge of baby oil. Since scent is the strongest memory, I know that should I smell it again, I would be knocked squarely back into such a time as this.

When I entered this bookstore, I stepped into a magical emporium of used books. Some were loved well. Some not so much. The strange rooms seemed to bloom like mushrooms, stocked with everything from rare signed first editions to ephemera collections from the early 1900s. A six-foot-high stack of romance novels snuggled up against a shelf of biographies of Frank Sinatra, Judy Garland, Mikhail Baryshnikov, and General Patton, which leaned against a plethora of 1960s magazines and maps from bygone eras. Think of Willy Wonka's Chocolate Factory, only with books. The Outer Banks bookstore was a maze of amazement and a boon to my soul during those lonely days—and, honestly, in the ensuing years. Every trip I took to the Banks was marked with at least three separate visits to the Outer Banks bookstore.

On one of my first days there in 1998, I veered to the restroom. As I wove behind a tall shelf filled with signed first editions, I noticed a short, semiconcealed shelf I had not seen before. Something about the relatively thin and short profile of many of the books there caught my eye. Even without bending down to get a closer look, I recognized them immediately—heavens, they were playscripts. I forgot all about the restroom (something I can no longer do as a woman of a certain age) and plopped down like a kid digging for diamonds in the dirt.

On the shelf were some of the modern usual suspects, to be sure, but wedged between those were plays I had never heard of from the early twentieth century. Some even had fading marks of the actor's trade: blocking notes, director's notes, and rehearsal call times. As an actor, I instantly knew what I was looking at. Though most of those actors were probably long gone from the earth, I cradled something in my hands that they had also cradled in theirs.

As I flipped through the yellowed pages, I imagined how they articulated their lines, the *click-clack* their shoes would have made walking the boards, the glory and agony that often accompanies the actor's trade. At the time of the discovery, I would have been bopping along to my iPod Shuffle while they would have been shuffling off to Buffalo.

Though the actors from those plays and I were separated by generations, the tools of the trade had not changed. Words and marks. Directions and choices. The element that formed an unbroken line from their era to mine was the script we had both held in our hands. And though the books had remained hidden for goodness knows how long, we would have both recognized the treasure I held in that Outer Banks strip mall. We would have both recognized the book we had, generations apart, held in our hands.

Sought

I sometimes wonder if Huldah had a similar experience. Huldah was a prophetess who stepped from relative obscurity (at least in the biblical record) into the scriptural spotlight. The drama of her life is contained in 2 Chronicles 34 and 2 Kings 22.

One day, a simple knock on a simple door—one question

to a largely unknown character—changed life all the way down through the ages, all the way to you and me. Here, I imagine her speaking to her husband, Shallum, part of the family who kept the king's wardrobe, after a sea change of a visit from some of the most powerful people in the land had occurred.

CONCEALED CHARACTERS

Huldah

You just missed them: Hilkiah. Ahikam. Abdon. Shaphan. Asaiah. If you hurry, you may still catch them. The high priest, the court secretary, in the young king's name. Yes, all of them were here in our home. There was no time to offer a meal, Shallum; they were not here for a meal. They carried the scroll with them, cradled as carefully as infant twins.

They nodded toward the scroll and told me that they found it while repairing the temple. Hilkiah took it, and then Shaphan read it in the young king's hearing. As the words poured over the king, he tore his clothing from neck to hem and commanded them, "Go and inquire of the LORD for me and for the remnant in Israel and Judah about what is written in this book that has been found. Great is the LORD's anger that is poured out on us because those who have gone before us have not kept the word of the LORD; they have not acted in accordance with all that is written in this book."

And so they came, saying that I must be consulted. I don't know why they never considered another to render judgment,

210

when even Hilkiah had recognized the words of the Lord.

It was found in the crumbling wall of the room where the silver had been kept. Lost as any child's bauble or workman's rag. Upon the common wood, they unfurled it one by one by one. They unfurled the holy words of the Holy One.

I wanted to trace the shape of them, but I dared not. I wanted to digest the marrow of them, but I dared not. For what seemed like Yahweh's own eternity, I stood soundless, so still that I felt like a statue. Only my eyes moved over and over the same words:

> Because you did not serve the LORD your God joyfully and gladly in the time of prosperity, therefore in hunger and thirst, in nakedness and dire poverty, you will serve the enemies the LORD sends against you. He will put an iron yoke on your neck until he has destroyed you.
>
> The LORD will bring a nation against you from far away, from the ends of the earth, like an eagle swooping down, a nation whose language you will not understand, a fierce-looking nation without respect for the old or pity for the young.

They were the words of Moses, the preeminent. Words that came back from the ages. Warnings, before we were to enter our land of promise. Warnings we have in no way heeded.

I didn't realize I was muttering the sage's words under my breath until the high priest said, "Well, then—Huldah? Do you agree? The king awaits an answer to his inquiry about these words. What do you say regarding them?"

I looked at the leaders of the realm, my voice as strong as an ancient oak, and told them to inform the king that disaster would indeed come, as sure as the dawn, much as we would give our very lives—for our children's sakes—to avoid it.

Captivity will come. God's patience, thirty years long, has reached its last breaths. The King of heaven's wave is coming in. I told them to tell the king that because he responded rightly to the words of God, he will be spared. He will be honored. He will have a long life.

I never thought I would wake to this day: the lost words of God have been found!

If I never speak another intelligible word upon the earth, this—and this alone—is what I was put upon the earth to do.

I told them to tell the king the words are exactly what they seem.

Shallum, I am tired. My words have finally emptied out.[1]

Huldah's story is easy to skip a rock across; in 2 Chronicles, it takes up a mere half chapter of real estate. But to pass over it would mean missing the depth of the water underneath.

One of the loudest notes in Huldah's story, aside from her affirmation of the words on the scroll as the words of God, is that the most powerful men in the land (including the high priest Hilkiah) went immediately to Huldah as the place of inquiry and validation. Her opinion was seen as definitive. Even with other high-powered people in the retinue, her voice mattered here, and she was absolutely unshy about using it for the Lord of glory. By prophesying that the words would come to pass and that young

King Josiah had responded correctly to these by mourning, she was affirming the veracity and the Source of the words.[2]

The Word of God had been lost but was now found.

Many scholars believe the lost and found scroll was part—or even the entirety—of the book of Deuteronomy.[3] Other scholars believe that Huldah was consulted, at least in part, to begin assembling what would become the canonized (or recognized) Old Testament.[4]

When King Josiah heard the affirmation from Huldah, a heart-rending, idolatry-leveling revival broke out, the likes of which hadn't been seen in Israel for eons. The Passover was observed again. The ark was returned to its rightful position and stature. Revival rain was finally falling on a land whose spiritual ground had been hard as iron. Commentator Michael Wilcock explains it this way: "It was an occasion unique in the whole history of the monarchy."[5]

Huldah's hidden heroism takes up only a handful of verses in the two places in which it occurs, yet Huldah's obedience changed history, and she played an outsized role in God's grand narrative— one that is still being parsed and examined by scholars for what it meant then and for what it might mean now. She was a woman soaked in the scent of freedom. Freedom to step into the moment joyfully, confidently, purposefully. For such a time as that.

A woman named Huldah. What treasures her hidden story gives to me.

A Huldah Heart

Recently, I had the honor of listening to a pioneering missionary whose name I cannot give (but whose permission I have to share this story). This minister has, to date, more than four thousand churches directly related to his ministry. His prayer from the time he met Jesus? "Lord, give me high impact and low visibility."

Sit with that for moment. *High impact. Low visibility.*

I wrote his prayer in the margins of my Bible and underscored it as if it were a password to the riches of heaven itself. In many ways, I suppose it is. Imagine the concentric ripples of four thousand churches on the earth—many of them in places where they ought not flourish—breathing and living and filling this world with the aroma of Christ (2 Corinthians 2:14–15).

One day, we will get to heaven and marvel together about what God did through one man who never cared about making a name for himself—who purposefully ran from making a name for himself—but who was consumed with the name and fame of Another. And whose very prayer was, "Keep me hidden, Lord, that I might be potent." At the end of his talk, everyone leaped to their feet, but it was a different kind of ovation. I've raved at ovations trumpeting the gift on display, and a time or two, I've even been a part of receiving them. But the sound of this ovation was different. It was a song of praise for the Giver, for the King, for the ways of the kingdom.

High impact, low visibility. What a prayer to pray. What a way to live. Free and flourishing.

The Spotlight, Then Holy Shadows

God has always intended His family to live with freedom. Paul referenced it in Romans 8 as he described God's coming design for all He has made: "Creation itself will also be set free from the bondage to decay into *the glorious freedom of God's children*" (v. 21 csb). This is God's transformational plan for creation and humanity.

Paul's experience of freedom as a servant of Jesus looked different from one season to the next—sometimes abounding, sometimes abasing.

The apostle abounded, giving compelling speeches on significant stages. He debated with philosophers in Athens and eloquently taught the truth of the gospel on Mars Hill. Then the apostle abased, spending long days in prison, sometimes awaiting trial. And while he was in Rome's Mamertine Prison, also known as the "House of Darkness," he wrote letters that would go on to theologically ground believers for centuries, even to this day.

Visible. Invisible. Revealed. Concealed.

Whether ministering in public visibility or in complete invisibility, Paul was faithful to the call, writing in the darkest of human circumstances the words that have formed the initial foundation of this bookish journey: "Set your minds on things above, not on things below. For you have died [Paul's own death was likely imminent], and your life is now hidden with Christ in God" (Colossians 3:2–3, paraphrase). Jesus was his treasure. Jesus was his glorious freedom. Jesus was more than enough, no matter the circumstances—thousands of eyes upon him, or none. He was completely secure in the view of his heavenly Father, in whom he was hidden.

Paul's example and words remind me to anchor myself in the glorious freedom of the children of God in an openhanded posture. Surrendered commitment. An enduring sense of, *However, whenever, whatever, whoever, wherever, Lord. Knowing that I am seen by You trumps every other consideration. So take me where You're working and do what You want through me.*

I've seen how faithfulness can look different in different seasons for others too. There is a lovely woman I know who is endowed with all the gifts one needs to stand on all the stages. She can sing and preach down the roof. She seems innately meant to be seen by human eyes, and she has certainly had seasons where she was.

But the call has changed for her of late, as she and her family prepare to go into hidden places to preach the Best News in All the World to those currently cut off from its sound. She's delighted to be following Jesus into this new chapter of life.

One season: the spotlight. The next: the holy shadows.

Like fall chooses to surrender to winter, and winter chooses to surrender to spring, my friend chooses to surrender to the season God has chosen for her, transforming with each. And in the choosing she is made and remade, free. Free to follow. Free to move. Free.

The Ebb and Flow

I, too, understand learning to trust God with the undulating ebb and flow of the rhythms of my life. Though I spent long years of my life as a musical theatre performer, due to some new physical limitations, that is no longer realistic for me. Oh, I can still manage pieces that don't demand sharp movement, but the days of crisp pirouettes and precise dance moves have gone the way of a wisp on the ocean wind.

I was recently asked by a former student turned friend to audition for a musical theatre piece that I have long desired to do. It was a plum union role; one that fit my vocal range and age. Most of all, I was over the moon at the possibility of sharing the stage with this dear, brilliant performer. Instinctually I said yes, heady with the possibility, and then . . . I remembered my new normal. After hemming and hawing, I reluctantly said, "Gosh, I don't think so," explaining the change in physical capability. Accepting my new reality was hard. Really, really hard.

But several days later, I began ponder: *Okay, hard as it is, you need to face it down. Sit with it. That chapter has closed, yes. But its end does not negate its value. And it does not mean nothing of value is ahead. What chapter might open next? How might I feel alive in my gifting in a new way?*

As I sit writing the close of this book, this I know: I serve an inexhaustible God—One who is not limited by my limitations. He never quits using the very gifts He has given to us, even if the form in which they are used changes.

> **I serve an inexhaustible God—One who is not limited by my limitations.**

Accepting this has brought me a freedom I had not previously experienced. Some kind of ending precedes every beginning. What we have always done is not what we will always do. But that doesn't mean there aren't still wonderful things *to do*.

Not until now have I stood so fully upon the ocean bank of my life and been thankful for the ebb and flow, in equal measure. Holy spotlight. Holy shadow.

While packing up the contents of our lives as we prepare to move, answering the call to a new season, I found one of those scripts from the Outer Banks bookstore. It was yellow and crumbling, its binding bent and broken, but the words were still clear as day. They articulated a language I still comprehend, though my days onstage as an actor are likely long gone. The words remind and rewind me. I still recognized them.

As I looked at those pages, I wasn't overcome with a sense of loss as if they were painful reminders, connected to my truest, most valuable self I can no longer reach. By His grace, not at all. Instead, my soul settled into the reality that my identity and value are established apart from all those years of performing. I am free to be on the stage *and* off the stage. I am free to enter into the story when destiny comes knocking, and I am free to step back into the wings when that assignment is done. Ebb and flow. Flow and ebb.

Faithfulness is up to me; fruitfulness is up to Him.

What I have done or been is not what I will always do or be. How delightfully liberating to move with the current of His leading and provision.

The driving pressure to perform, the dopamine hits of exposure—none of those things is more real than heaven and heaven's King. Faithfulness is up to me; fruitfulness is up to Him. He gets to choose the outcome of that faithfulness. And, in His choosing, I am made and remade—free.

Jesus,

I feel freedom in deepening ways. In deepening places. From the ocean floor and the riptides that have tried to undo me, to the places I have struggled and sought to be seen by human eyes, turning from Your eyes—the ones that can make me, root me, secure me.

Your eyes roam the earth seeking to encourage those whose hearts are fully committed to You. I know my heart is wily and wonky, but it also is something You have made and shaped and reshaped. So, Lord, here again, I say: it's Yours.

Though I know there are miles to go, I receive into my heart afresh Your seeing, Your knowing, Your freeing.

Now, Lord, let's walk. Let's walk on.

Hidden Rhythms

Your life is now hidden with Christ in God.

COLOSSIANS 3:3

During the quarter century that my family has been retreating to the Outer Banks, as much has changed as has stayed the same. Favorite haunts, like the used bookstore, have shuttered. Hurricanes have shaped and reshaped the shoreline. What was once a hidden jewel has been held up to the light as people now come from all over to discover its wild beauty.

Jonathan and I have gone from newlyweds to the parents of two sons. Jonathan's brother and his wife have followed suit. During those years we've lost precious beloveds: Gigi Ma and my mother, Patsy Crout, among them. Pop, the patriarch who began our family's rhythm of retreating to the Banks, has walked through difficult bouts of cancer; the most recent one forced him to forego his beloved Outer Banks. Thankfully, last year, he returned.

We've walked through more topsy-turvy seasons than I could enumerate here: glorious peeks inside the kingdom's delights and front-row seats to its difficulties. Physically, I see the fluctuations too—some bodies are breaking down among us, and some bodies are only just beginning to flourish.

Ebb and flow. Flow and Ebb.

Advance. Retreat.

Rushing out. Rushing in.

Tides.

This is the way of things. Where there is life, there is change.

During seasons of upheaval, stable rhythms matter. Walks at dusk. She-crab soup at Sam and Omie's. Puzzles strewn about the big table. John's milkshakes. Rainy-day movies. The aquarium. Jennette's pier. The Cape Hatteras Lighthouse. Manteo ice cream. Crab-gazing at night. The Lost Colony. Watching for dolphins. Feeding seagulls the last of leftover bread. The slow, soft sadness that descends the day before we pack our belongings and return to life without salted air or sanded wind.

> **This is the way of things. Where there is life, there is change.**

In a few short weeks my family will return to Kill Devil Hills, near Kitty Hawk, where the Wright Brothers roped the wind and ripped the sky with their first flight. We'll return to the same beach I combed and happened upon the black whelk, the symbol that began to codify the musings that had been wind wisps in my ears for years.

Has the hidden-with-Christ life become more real? Less real? Am I the same?

Oh, what a year can do. And what it can't.

In many ways our family's desolate night has tipped its hat to a rising light. The beams are dim, fogged in by a retreating storm, but obscurity is surrendering. I imagine ancient mariners, battered and bullied by the maelstrom, gaining their sea legs again; raising their chins to something greater, cutting through the storm. I picture the lighthouses—Bodie Island, Cape Hatteras, Currituck Beach—that dot the jagged banks of the barrier islands. Immovable, resolute, tall, battered, purposeful. I see grizzled faces turning for land, for hidden havens. They navigate in, as my family does, changed. Parts of us are baby-skin new, while others are calloused—our hands blistered from lashing our spiritual ropes around the mast that is Jesus.

Somehow, we see that our mast has held firm through the storm. To His name I bind myself forever. Though the sails are shot through and we will now need to raise new ones, we *know*—beyond the shadows that doubt casts—that there is hope. We know that we are hidden eternally with Christ in a God who sees around corners.

We did not know this a year ago. At the time, we were facing a season of full-life unknowns—lifelong calling, lifelong friendships, life's long history—too many losses to enumerate or ameliorate. But we know that our God knows us.

There is a delicious freedom in knowing that because He sees us, secures us, and frees us, we are truly unbound.

> There is a delicious freedom in knowing that because He sees us, secures us, and frees us, we are truly unbound.

Conclusion

Free to choose the hidden-with-Christ life.

Free to cultivate a heart that no longer fights for anything else other than rejoicing in being one of His own.

Known by name.

Seen and beloved.

Secure and free.

A Faithful Heart

I ruminated about which Concealed Character I would like to take a final walk down the beach accompanied by. I hemmed and hawed and dreamed and mused, and then I happened upon a church history book and bumped into a hidden encounter that changed the genesis of the early church.

CONCEALED CHARACTERS

J. M.

I walked the beach that day. I circled and circled over again the philosophies that had bounded my life as tight as a sandal strap. Plato said that to glimpse God was to dive as deep into truth as if plumbing the depths of the ocean. At the end of such a dive would be revelation, epiphany, insight. Hidden gems for the brave and bold and brilliant. And treasure in hand, I could

Conclusion

surface, complete. I could exit the circle of Plato and enter the forum of the Stoics, the acuities of Aristotle. Great men on whom I patterned my life, my thought, my time. From one shelf of philosophy to another, one tome to another. One footfall and then another. And another.

And then him.

At first, I saw an outline of flesh and bone. The sun backlighting glory. Aged. Leathery. Brown as the leather of a shoe. He was elderly but dignified. Stepping without hurry but with purpose, joy. Joy let loose.

He waved me to his side, and we walked together. He asked what I had been puzzling over. For some reason, my citadels fell, and I spoke of the conundrum of Plato's promise. What truth should be plumbed? How would we know when we had gone as deeply as we should have? I spoke for hours on end as we walked the beach, the waves ebbing and flowing near our feet.

When my words ran dry as a dead well, the old man by the sea spoke. He said truth was not a problem to be solved but a Person to be loved—named Jesus. I had heard whispers of Him, but only as another thinker, philosopher. This man—honorable and dignified—explained to me a better way. He spoke of the prophecies of old, showing that Jesus was the true expression of God.

My whole life—the writings, the meetings with great minds expressing the goodness of God Himself—all of this was because an unknown man by the sea spoke, and I listened.

I never did get his name.

Conclusion

This is an extrapolation of the account given by Justin Martyr, the church's first great apologist (defender of the faith) and one of its first martyrs. Martyr reportedly said before his death, "You can kill us, but you cannot do us any real harm."

Martyr's ministry moves across the ages. He began to defend the faith at the outset of the church age. And his entire life was changed by an encounter with an anonymous man on the beach.

I want to be like the man on the beach that day: a hidden gem in God's hand, found by grace and used for His purposes. I want to recline into the knowledge that what we do for Him echoes through all eternity. These things are the things that remain.

What if we allowed the Lord to purge us of the drive for visibility or fame and instead sought a faithful heart? What if we showed up to the moment the Lord presented to us, stepping into the spotlight of the story and then fading away into obscurity if that was God's call upon us? What if we courted contentment and ran fully into the great adventure with Jesus, unfettered by the drive to be known and seen by human eyes, but rather to be known and seen by God and to be fully satiated in this glorious truth?

Sea Glass

During the summers we've been traveling to the Outer Banks, I began to hear about a different kind of beachcomber. These determined searchers weren't looking for the rare whole shell; they were hunting for sea glass. I'd heard of sea glass for years, but all of a sudden I was seeing books about sea glass, necklaces made of sea glass, and art made up of sea glass. The rabid trend seemed to come out of nowhere.

Except sea glass doesn't really come from nowhere. Sea glass is glass or china that has been tumbled in the sea for who knows how many years, the rough edges worn away by the waves, the colors polished to a high shine. I've seen what I am sure are bits of common, brown glass bottles sea-shined until they look like gleaming pieces of amber, beautiful enough for the centerpiece of a necklace. Though I've never found one myself, pieces of china from the 1600s and 1700s that would take your breath away with their unusual vintage patterns have been found. Usually these treasures are found in the early morning, when the tide retreats. These sea jewels are rare and beautiful, highly prized and coveted.

Whenever I find a rare piece of sea glass at my beloved Outer Banks, I pause and cradle it in my hand. I think of the rough-and-tumble polishing. I think of the years and years of hiddenness that made it shine. I think of the transformative power of life in the hidden place, and, in this, I treasure the transformation of the sea. I think back on my discovery of the black whelk and the hidden-with-Christ life it led me to.

I close my fist around the sea glass, my hidden gem. I want you to sense those spiritual treasures in your palm as well. Gifts from God. I want you to search for them, grasp them, and hold on to them. Be changed by them. I want you to believe that because your Beholder sees you, your value to Him is unquestionable.

I want you to relax into the truth that you are "hidden with God in Christ"—*nothing* can remove you from His hand. From that place of eternal safety and security, you are invited to dance on the shoreline. To delight in being delighted in. To live free.

Then may you allow that delight and freedom to spill over into a bruised and sore world. (We need you out here.)

Lean into these life-changing gifts, friend. And keep looking up to the One who sees you as you walk the ocean's edge all the way home.

Acknowledgments

Little is harder than codifying all those who stewarded and midwifed a work; there is always the nagging sense that someone is being overlooked. However, that never quite stops the attempt across the high wire, clumsy though it may be.

Jonathan, Levi, Luke, Dad and Jan, Jetta and Jim, Ev and Jim, and my South Carolina family: you have remained the taproots of my life.

Lease, Constant, Aid, Shanone, and Heather: you form a mighty quintet of hope.

Dr. Jim Howard, (almost) Dr. Lisa Harper, Dr. Lynn Cohick, Scott Lindsey: your generosity of spirit, intellect, and insight finds a grateful beneficiary here.

Sara Riemersma: thank you for seeing the value of this work, even before I fully did. I'm gratefully indebted to you for the way you see.

Carrie Marrs: thank you for stewarding my wonky heart and wobbly words with abundant grace. I'm stunned by your gifts.

Acknowledgments

The W team and the whole HarperCollins team: y'all embody the phrase, "All is grace."

Lisa Jackson, thank you for an unwavering hand and heart.

Rhodes, Prays, Williamses, Guptills, Coxes, Spencers—thank you.

The body of Christ: in the maelstrom, in the storm, thank you for allowing God to fill your sails with grace, forgiveness, and a life that looks like the gospel on display.

Notes

Chapter 1

1. Lori M. Nichols, "11 Fascinating Facts about Shells and Other Things You Find on N.J. Beaches," NJ.com, August 15, 2017, https://www.nj.com/entertainment/2017/08/fun_facts_about_shells.html.

2. José H. Leal, "Nature's Iron-Based Shell Dye." Bailey-Matthews National Shell Museum & Aquarium, August 28, 2020. https://www.shellmuseum.org/post/nature-s-iron-based-shell-dye#:~:text=In%20sand%20or%20mud%20with,shells%20with%20unusually%20dark%20hues.

3. Craig S. Keener, *The IVP Bible Background Commentary: New Testament*, 2nd ed. (Downers Grove, IL: IVP Academic, 2014), 200.

4. Richard R. Losch, *All the People in the Bible: An A–Z Guide to the Saints, Scoundrels, and Other Characters in Scripture* (Grand Rapids, MI: William B. Eerdmans, 2008), 153–54, 218; William Smith, s.v. "Tiberius," in *Smith's Bible Dictionary*, rev. F. N. and M. A. Peloubet (Grand Rapids, MI: Zondervan, 1967); Allison A. Trites in *The Gospel of Luke, Acts*, Cornerstone Biblical Commentary, vol. 12 (Carol Stream, IL: Tyndale House Publishers, 2006), 127–28; Ben Witherington III, "Joanna (Person)," in *The Anchor Yale Bible Dictionary*, ed. David Noel Freedman (New York: Doubleday, 1992), 855; Samuel Terrien, *Till the Heart Sings: A Biblical Theology of Manhood and Womanhood* (Grand Rapids, MI: William B. Eerdmans Publishing Company, 2004), 123; *ESV Study Bible* (Wheaton, IL: Crossway, 2008), 1967.

Notes

5. Gary V. Smith, *Ezra-Nehemiah,* in *Ezra, Nehemiah, Esther,* Cornerstone Biblical Commentary, vol. 5b (Carol Stream, IL: Tyndale House Publishers, 2010), 123; Mervin Breneman, *Ezra, Nehemiah, Esther,* The New American Commentary, vol. 10 (Nashville, TN: B&H Publishing Group, 1993), 189. Allison Allen with Ashley Wiersma, *Hidden Video Study: Finding Delight in Your Life With Christ* (Grand Rapids, MI: Zondervan, 2023), DVD.

> Some scholars posit that Shallum had no sons to join the work and so chose his daughters to join him, but whatever the reason, we see that it is Shallum's daughters that help their father rebuild the wall. **3:9–12 Rephaiah . . . Shallum.** Similar to the list of faithful people in Hebrews 11, this chapter carefully chronicles the names of the faithful people who rebuilt the walls of Jerusalem. Although one might expect political officials to be directing others, two leaders of districts within Jerusalem (Rephaiah and Shallum) took on the manual labor of repairing a portion of the wall. The dedication of these people was remarkable. I imagine these daughters of Shallum to be women of renown and wealth **3:12** "Shallum," as was Rephaiah in v. 9, was ruler of part of the countryside around Jerusalem. Scholar Gary V. Smith writes, "Some understand *bĕnôt,* 'daughters,' as 'small towns' and translate 'he and men from small towns.'" It is true that *bĕnôt* is used of "daughter" towns, but here the masculine suffix argues for the NIV translation. If Shallum had no sons, his daughters would have inherited his property (Num 27:1–11). This mention of women involved in the work again demonstrates the extent of Nehemiah's support and his mobilization of the people.

6. Derek Kidner, "Commentary on Isaiah," in *New Bible Commentary,* 4th ed. Edited by D. A. Carson et al. (Downers Grove, IL: IVP Academic, 1994), 659.

Chapter 2

1. Claire Ferguson, "Scaphella Junonia," *Beach Combing,* April 21, 2023, https://www.beachcombingmagazine.com/blogs/news/scaphella-junonia.
2. Mark H. Bickel, "After Years of Searching, Fort Myers Man Finally Finds Rare Shell on Sanibel Island," *Fort Myers News-Press,* May 23, 2023, https://www.news-press.com/story/news/local/2023/05/20/rare-junonia-shell-found-on-sanibel-island-florida-beach/70220358007/.

Notes

3. Connie Leinbach, "N.C. Shell Club Member Finds Record-Breaking Scotch Bonnet," *Ocracoke Observer*, April 10, 2022, https://ocracokeobserver.com/2022/04/10/n-c-shell-club-member-finds-record-breaking-scotch-bonnet/.

4. "Ocracoke School," Ocracoke Navigator, accessed September 10, 2023, https://www.ocracokenavigator.com/ocracoke-school.

5. In the legal custom of the day, a barren woman could give her maidservant to her husband as a slave wife and the child that would be born to that union would be regarded as the first wife's child. If the husband then declared in public that the child of the slave wife was his son, then that son would be adopted as the heir. So Sarai's suggestion was unobjectionable according to the customs of the day, but God often repudiates social customs, especially if they interfere with his wonderful works.

   Allen Ross, *Genesis,* in *Genesis, Exodus*, Cornerstone Biblical Commentary, vol. 1 (Carol Stream, IL: Tyndale House Publishers, 2008), 116; Andrew E. Steinmann, *Genesis: An Introduction and Commentary*, Tyndale Old Testament Commentaries, vol. 1 (Downers Grove, IL: IVP Academic, 2019), 173.

6. D. A. Carson et al., eds., *New Bible Commentary*, 4th ed. (Downers Grove, IL: IVP, 1994), 72.

7. Matthew D. Montonini, s.v. "Theophany," in *The Lexham Bible Dictionary*, ed. John D. Barry et al. (Bellingham, WA: Lexham Press, 2016).

8. H. D. M. Spence and Joseph S. Excell, eds., *The Pulpit Commentary: Genesis*, reprint ed. (Grand Rapids, MI: William B. Eerdmans, 1978), 228.

9. William Smith, s.v. "Selah," *Smith's Bible Dictionary*, rev. F. N. and M. A. Peloubet (Grand Rapids, MI: Zondervan, 1967).

10. Kandy Queen-Sutherland, s.v. "Naming," in *Holman Illustrated Bible Dictionary*, ed. Chad Brand et al. (Nashville, TN: Holman Bible Publishers, 2003).

11. Craig S. Keener, *The IVP Bible Background Commentary: New Testament*, 2nd ed. (Downers Grove, IL: IVP Academic, 1993), 771; Horst Balz and Gerhard Schneider, eds., *Exegetical Dictionary of the New Testament*, vol. 2 (Grand Rapids, MI: William B. Eerdmans, 1991), 519.

12. Carson et al., *New Bible Commentary*, 72–73.

13. Michelle J. Morris, s.v. "Hagar," in *The Lexham Bible Dictionary*, ed. John D. Barry et al. (Bellingham, WA: Lexham Press, 2016).

14. Carson et al., *New Bible Commentary*.

15. Robert W. Jenson, *A Theology in Outline: Can These Bones Live?* ed. Adam Eitel (New York: Oxford University Press, 2016), 15.

16. The lengthiest one-on-one conversation Jesus had with anyone, man or woman, was with the Samaritan woman at the well in John 4. When Jesus' disciples returned from a trip to get vittles, they "were surprised to find him *talking with a woman*. But no one asked him, 'What do you want?' or 'Why are you talking with her?'" (v. 27). Five thousand years after God's desert encounter with Hagar, it was still perceived as unusual for God to talk with a woman and invite a woman to dialogue with Him.

17. "Does the Old Testament Dehumanize Women? Dr. Sandy Richter (Exiles 22 Talk + Q & A)," YouTube video, February 9, 2023, 0:01, https://www .youtube.com/watch?v=AjnMM36QUjA. Dr. Sandy Richter's speech is a fabulous resource for understanding the familial and societal structures we see represented in the Old Testament. I am indebted to her teaching on this subject, as it helped inform my understanding of Hagar's state.

18. If you or someone you know is the victim of abuse, I strongly urge you to seek safety and help from trusted experts. Following are some resources, which can be part of meeting your physical, psychological, and spiritual needs. https://www.thehotline.org/; https://www.benefits.gov/news /article/472; 1-800-799-SAFE.

Chapter 3

1. "The Lost Colony," The Lost Colony, accessed September 13, 2023, https://www.thelostcolony.org/the-lost-colony.

2. James Horn, "The Roanake Colonies," First Colony Foundation, accessed September 13, 2023, https://www.firstcolonyfoundation.org/history/the -roanoke-colonies/; Brendan Wolfe, "The Roanoke Colonies," Encyclopedia Virginia, accessed September 13, 2023, https:// encyclopediavirginia.org/entries/roanoke-colonies-the/; Mike Baker, "Lost Colony Enthusiasts Discover Few Clues in a Swamp," *LA Times*, September 30, 2007, https://www.latimes.com/archives/la-xpm-2007-sep -30-adna-lost30-story.html.

3. Clinton E. Arnold, "Plans Underway to Excavate Colossae," *The Good Book Blog*, Biola University, February 3, 2022, https://www.biola.edu /blogs/good-book-blog/2022/plans-underway-to-excavate-colossae.

4. D. A. Carson et al., eds., *New Bible Commentary*, 4th ed. (Downers Grove, IL: IVP, 1994), 1260.

5. Craig S. Keener, *The IVP Bible Background Commentary: New Testament*, 2nd ed. (Downers Grove, IL: IVP Academic, 1993), 568–70.

6. *ESV Study Bible* (Wheaton, IL: Crossway, 2008), 2993.
7. Carson et al., *New Bible Commentary*, 1260–63.
8. Brittney Miller, "Florida's Algae Problem: What Is It, and How Can It Affect You?" Florida Museum, June 15, 2021, https://www.floridamuseum .ufl.edu/earth-systems/blog/floridas-algae-problem-what-is-it-and-how -can-it-affect-you/.
9. Hermann Olshausen, *Biblical Commentary on the New Testament*, vol. 6, rev. A. C. Kendrick (New York: Sheldon, Blakeman & Co., 1858), 257.
10. Clinton E. Arnold, *The Colossian Syncretism: The Interface Between Christianity and Folk Belief at Colossae* (Eugene, OR: Wipf & Stock, 2014); See also Keener, *The IVP Bible Background Commentary*, 568–82.
11. H. D. M. Spence and Joseph S. Excell, eds., introduction to *The Pulpit Commentary: Colossians*, reprint ed. (Grand Rapids, MI: William B. Eerdmans, 1978).
12. Johannes P. Louw and Eugene Albert Nida, *Greek-English Lexicon of the New Testament: Based on Semantic Domains* (New York: United Bible Societies, 1996), 259.
13. Arnold, *The Colossian Syncretism*.
14. E. Stanley Jones, *In Christ: 364 Meditations on Passages from the New Testament* (New York: Abingdon Press, 1961), 9.
15. Jones, *In Christ*, 101.
16. Bible Hub, s.v. "sun," accessed September 13, 2023, https://biblehub.com /greek/4862.htm.
17. Smith, *Smith's Bible Dictionary*, s.v. "Meals."
18. Horst Balz and Gerhard Schneider, eds., *Exegetical Dictionary of the New Testament*, vol. 2 (Grand Rapids, MI: William B. Eerdmans, 1991), 322–24.
19. Peter Vankevich, "Was 'The Lost Colony' Really Lost or Just Decamped to Hatteras Island?" *Island Free Press*, December 28, 2020, https:// islandfreepress.org/hatteras-island-features/was-the-lost-colony-really-lost -or-just-decamped-to-hatteras-island/.
20. I must offer a huge debt of thanks to Dr. Lynn Cohick for reading this chapter and offering help. And, though she eschews said thanks, she must receive them nonetheless. Many thanks also to Dr. Jim Howard for his helpful conversations about Colossians.

Chapter 4

1. "Freedmen, Surfmen, Heroes: Richard Etheridge and Surfmen of the Pea Island Station," Pea Island Preservation Society, Inc., accessed September 13, 2023, https://www.peaislandpreservationsociety.com/;

Notes

Historian's Office, United States Coast Guard. "The Long Blue Line: Keeper
Richard Etheridge and the Gold Medal Lifesavers of Pea Island." United
States Coast Guard, February 3, 2023. https://www.mycg.uscg.mil/News
/Article/3259413/the-long-blue-line-keeper-richard-etheridge-and-the-gold
-medal-lifesavers-of-pe/.

2. G. Walter Hansen, *Galatians*, The IVP New Testament Commentary
Series (Downers Grove, IL: InterVarsity Press, 1994), Ga 1:18–24.

3. H. D. M. Spence and Joseph S. Excell, eds., *The Pulpit Commentary:
Exodus,* vol. 1, reprint ed. (Grand Rapids, MI: William B. Eerdmans,
1978), 37.

4. T. D. Alexander, in *New Bible Commentary,* ed. D. A. Carson et al., 4th
ed. (Downers Grove, IL: IVP, 1994), 96.

5. J. Ramsey Michaels, *Hebrews,* in *1 Timothy, 2 Timothy, Titus, Hebrews,*
Cornerstone Biblical Commentary, vol. 17 (Carol Stream, IL: Tyndale
House Publishers, 2009), 430.

6. Thomas D. Lea, *Hebrews & James,* Holman New Testament Commentary,
vol. 10 (Nashville, TN: Holman Reference, 1999), 204.

7. Among scholars there is some difference in thought as to whether
Jethro/Reuel would have worshiped foreign gods, especially as he later
worships Yahweh. Some believe he worshiped foreign gods, as the
Midianites were known to do. Ricky L. Johnson, s.v. "Midian,
Midianites," in *Holman Bible Dictionary*, StudyLight, accessed
October 14, 2023, https://www.studylight.org/dictionaries/eng/hbd/m
/midian-midianites.html. In writing Zipporah's Concealed Character
narrative, I chose to lean toward Jethro being a pagan priest at Moses'
entrance into their story. For instance, we see pagan mothers of the
heads of the twelve tribes of Israel, and we see formerly pagan women,
including Bathsheba (former wife of a Hittite), Rahab, and Ruth
the Moabitess.

8. Rob Fleenor, s.v. "Midianites," in *The Lexham Bible Dictionary*, ed. John
D. Barry et al. (Bellingham, WA: Lexham Press, 2016).

9. T. D. Alexander, *New Bible Commentary*, 98.

10. *Brown-Driver-Briggs*, s.v. "qatan," Bible Hub, accessed September 13, 2023,
https://biblehub.com/hebrew/6996.htm.

11. Guy Winch, "10 Surprising Facts About Rejection," *Psychology Today*,
July 3, 2013, https://www.psychologytoday.com/us/blog/the-squeaky
-wheel/201307/10-surprising-facts-about-rejection.

12. Historian's Office, United States Coast Guard "The Long Blue Line:
Keeper Richard Etheridge and the Gold Medal Lifesavers of Pea Island,"

Notes

My CG, US Coast Guard, February 3, 2023, https://www.mycg.uscg.mil/News/Article/3259413/the-long-blue-line-keeper-richard-etheridge-and-the-gold-medal-lifesavers-of-pe/.

Chapter 5

1. "Rip Currents," North Carolina Sea Grant, accessed September 13, 2023, https://ncseagrant.ncsu.edu/rip-currents/.
2. Allison Allen, *Requiem* (unpublished manuscript, 2011).
3. Craig S. Keener, *The IVP Bible Background Commentary: New Testament*, 2nd ed. (Downers Grove, IL: IVP Academic, 1993), 427; Craig Keener, *The Bible Background Commentary* (Downers Grove, IL: IVP, 1993).
4. "Surgeon General Issues New Advisory About Effects Social Media Use Has on Youth Mental Health," US Department of Health and Human Services, May 23, 2023, https://www.hhs.gov/about/news/2023/05/23/surgeon-general-issues-new-advisory-about-effects-social-media-use-has-youth-mental-health.html.
5. "Surgeon General Issues New Advisory."
6. H. D. M. Spence and Joseph S. Excell, eds., *The Pulpit Commentary: Isaiah,* reprint ed. (Grand Rapids, MI: William B. Eerdmans, 1978); J. Alec Motyer, *Isaiah: An Introduction and Commentary*, Tyndale Old Testament Commentaries, vol. 20 (Downers Grove, IL: InterVarsity Press, 1999), 293.
7. Christine Liebrecht, Lettica Hustinx, and Margot van Mulken, "The Relative Power of Negativity: The Influence of Language Intensity on Perceived Strength," *Journal of Language and Social Psychology* 38, no. 2 (March 2019): 170–93, https://doi.org/10.1177/0261927X18808562.

Chapter 6

1. Peter Tan-Gatue, s.v. "Scribe," in *The Lexham Bible Dictionary*, ed. John D. Barry et al. (Bellingham, WA: Lexham Press, 2016).

Chapter 7

1. Chris Blaha, "The Majestic OBX Live Oaks," Currituck County Center, NC Cooperative Extension, accessed September 13, 2023, https://currituck.ces.ncsu.edu/2020/05/the-majestic-obx-live-oaks/.
2. "Elizabethan Gardens," OuterBanks.com, accessed September 13, 2023, https://www.outerbanks.com/elizabethan-gardens.html.
3. Mark D. Futato, *The Book of Psalms* in *The Book of Psalms, The Book of Proverbs*, Cornerstone Biblical Commentary, vol. 7 (Carol Stream, IL:

237

Notes

Tyndale House Publishers, 2009), 299. I am thankful to Lisa Harper, who first drew my attention to this particular understanding of the word "planted" in this pslam on her podcast *Back Porch Theology*.

4. Allison Allen, *Thirsty for More: Discovering God's Uexpected Blessings in a Desert Season* (Grand Rapids, MI: Revell, 2017), 65–66.

5. Dale A. Brueggemann, *Numbers* in *Leviticus, Numbers, Deuteronomy*, Cornerstone Biblical Commentary, vol. 2 (Carol Stream, IL: Tyndale House Publishers, 1996), 329.

6. Donald K. Campbell, "Joshua," in *The Bible Knowledge Commentary: Old Testament*, vol. 1, ed. J. F. Walvoord and R. B. Zuck (Wheaton, IL: Victor Books, 1985), 336.

Chapter 8

1. "Solitary Dolphins," Project Jonah, accessed September 13, 2023, https://www.projectjonah.org.nz/solitary-dolphins/.

2. Laetitia Nunny and Mark P. Simmonds, "A Global Reassessment of Solitary-Sociable Dolphins," *Frontiers in Veterinary Science* 5 (2018), https://doi.org/10.3389/fvets.2018.00331.

3. Carrie Hodgin, "'I've Never Seen Them Do This,' Surfer Captures Dolphin Pod Riding the Waves in Outer Banks," WFMY News 2, June 30, 2020, https://www.wfmynews2.com/article/news/local/ive-never-seen-them-do-this-surfer-captures-dolphin-pod-riding-the-waves-in-outer-banks/83-b0d1498c-e5fd-4c50-b9d9-0e26aedc4aaf.

4. Allen P. Ross, "Psalms," in *The Bible Knowledge Commentary: An Exposition of the Scriptures*, ed. J. F. Walvoord and R. B. Zuck, vol. 1 (Wheaton, IL: Victor Books, 1985), 855.

5. Maya Margit, "Jerusalem's 2,000-Year-Old Pilgrimage Road Preparing for Modern Revival," *Jerusalem Post*, January 8, 2023, https://www.jpost.com/archaeology/article-726942.

6. Chad Brand et al., eds., in *Holman Illustrated Bible Dictionary* (Nashville, TN: Holman Bible Publishers, 2003), s.v. "Swallow."

7. J. A. Motyer, in *New Bible Commentary*, ed. D. A. Carson et al. (Downers Grove, IL: IVP, 1994), 540.

8. Allison Allen, "Building a Nest," *The Remarkable Blog*, March 25, 2016, http://rpmdaily.net/blog/building-a-nest.

Chapter 9

1. "Administrative Record for the Relocation of the Cape Hatteras Light Station, PC.5003," Outer Banks History Center, accessed September 13, 2023,

https://axaem.archives.ncdcr.gov/findingaids/PC_5003_Administrative
_Record_f_.html.

2. Stephanie Hall, "5 Shipwrecks You Can Visit Along the Outer Banks's
Coast," The Outer Banks of North Carolina, April 29, 2020, https://
www.outerbanks.org/blog/post/5-shipwrecks-you-can-visit-along
-the-outer-bankss-shoreline.

3. Abigail Tucker, "Did Archaeologists Uncover Blackbeard's Treasure?"
Smithsonian, March 2011, https://www.smithsonianmag.com/history
/did-archaeologists-uncover-blackbeards-treasure-215890/.

4. For example, Isaiah 59:2; Deuteronomy 31:17; Micah 3:4; Ezekiel 39:24.

5. *Strong's Concordance*, s.v. "halak," Bible Hub, accessed September 13, 2023,
https://biblehub.com/hebrew/1980.htm.

6. HELPS Word-Studies, s.v. "poreuomai," Bible Hub, accessed
September 13, 2023, https://biblehub.com/greek/4198.htm.

7. HELPS Word-Studies, s.v. "teleó," Bible Hub, accessed October 16, 2023,
https://biblehub.com/greek/5055.htm.

8. Martin Luther, "A Mighty Fortress," Hymnary.org, https://hymnary.org
/text/a_mighty_fortress_is_our_god_a_bulwark.

Chapter 11

1. Scriptures taken from John 3:2–7 esv and adapted from John 3:16. See
also Allison Allen, *Requiem* (unpublished manuscript, 2015).

2. Allison Allen, "The Great In-Between: A Good Friday Reflection," 2018.

3. Jonathan and Allison Allen, "I Don't Have to Know," 1998, Tall People
Music/ASCAP.

4. Mayo Clinic Staff, "Stages of Labor and Birth: Baby, It's Time!" Mayo
Clinic, accessed September 13, 2023, https://www.mayoclinic.org
/healthy-lifestyle/labor-and-delivery/in-depth/stages-of-labor/art
-20046545.

Chapter 12

1. Scripture quotations taken from 2 Chronicles 34:21 and
Deuteronomy 28:47–50.

2. Athalya Brenner-Idan, *The Israelite Woman: Social Role and Literary
Type in Biblical Narrative*, Cornerstones (New York: Bloomsbury, 2015),
60–61; Samuel Terrien, *Till the Heart Sings: A Biblical Theology of
Manhood and Womanhood* (Grand Rapids, MI: William B. Eerdmans,
2004), 81–82; Esther J. Hamori, *Women's Divination in Biblical
Literature: Prophecy, Necromancy, and Other Arts of Knowledge*, Anchor

Notes

Yale Bible Reference Library (New Haven, CT: Yale University Press, 2015), 152–53.

3. D. A. Carson et al., eds., *New Bible Commentary*, 4th ed. (Downers Grove, IL: IVP, 1994), 417.

4. Gerald E. Gerbrandt, *Deuteronomy*, ed. Douglas B. Miller, Loren L. Johns, and Elmer A. Martens, Believers Church Bible Commentary (Harrisonburg, VA; Kitchener, ON: Herald Press, 2015), 499.

5. Michael Wilcock, *New Bible Commentary*, ed. Carson et al., 148.

About the Author

Allison Allen has spent a lifetime walking in the shoes of others and champions the power of narrative to engage and restore the human heart. As a student, she was chosen as an Andrew Carnegie Scholar in the prestigious acting program at Carnegie Mellon University. After graduating from CMU, she landed on Broadway for two years in the original cast of the revival of *Grease*. Along the way she has written or cowritten numerous plays and musicals, as well as ministered with Women of Faith for three years as their dramatist.

She now uses her gifts to teach the Bible all over the country and loves nothing more than watching people run headlong into the freedom that Jesus offers. Of late, Allison has been tickled pink to be the five-foot-twelve spiritual wing-woman to Lisa Harper on the well-received podcast *Lisa Harper's Back Porch Theology*. Allison is the author of two previous books: *Shine: Stepping into the Role You Were Made For* and *Thirsty for More: Discovering God's Unexpected Blessings in a Desert Season*. Allison has been married to worship pastor Jonathan Allen for a quarter of a century. Together they have an old-covenant son and a new-covenant son, Levi and Luke.